*This Book Belongs To:*

*Christmas 2014*

# 2014 CHRISTMAS WITH Southern Living

# 2014 CHRISTMAS

WITH

# Southern Living

OUR BEST GUIDE TO HOLIDAY
COOKING & DECORATING

Oxmoor House®

# Welcome

There's just something magical about Christmas celebrations in the South. Whether it's the fragrant scent of fresh evergreen decorations draping the mantel, a loaf of bread baking in the oven, or a table set in anticipation of a cozy holiday dinner, these extra touches add to the festive feeling this time of year. *Christmas with Southern Living* invites you to ring in the holidays with some of our ideas for fabulous decorations, gracious entertaining, and easy-but-impressive gifts.

If you like to host spirited yuletide gatherings centered on family, friends, and food, look no further than these pages for ideas to make the season merry and bright. You'll find scrumptious menus that feature everything from a global-inspired cocktail party to an elegant dessert celebration complete with tablescape designs. Welcome holiday guests to your home with handcrafted decorations for the front door, mantel, and even some twists on the classic Christmas tree. Gather family and friends to savor and share the magic of the season with holiday dishes made a little bit easier with recipes for simple-to-bake breads, slow-cooker sides, no-fuss brownies, and more. And show them that you love them with from-the-heart gift ideas for sweets, savories, and even a little something extra.

As you prepare for this season of cherished traditions and merriment, we wish you a joyful holiday filled with all the wonderful gifts and pleasures it has to offer.

Susan

Susan Ray
EDITOR

# CONTENTS

## ENTERTAIN 8



## DECORATE 86



## SAVOR 104



## SHARE 138

# *Entertain*

# Bluegrass Brunch

*Who says that you have to cook fancy feasts during the holidays? Invite guests over for Kentucky-inspired cuisine that's steeped in tradition.*

THE MENU
Bluegrass Brunch
serves 10
KENTUCKY WINTER CHAMPAGNE COCKTAIL
CLASSIC MINT JULEP
OYSTER FRITTERS
HOT BROWN EGGS BENEDICT
KENTUCKY-STYLE SMOKED LEG OF LAMB
ROASTED ASPARAGUS WITH SHAVED PARMESAN
WINTER FRUIT COMPOTE
DECADENT CHOCOLATE-BOURBON PECAN PIE
SORGHUM-APPLE STACK CAKE

# KENTUCKY WINTER CHAMPAGNE COCKTAIL

**MAKES 12 SERVINGS**
**HANDS-ON 6 MIN.  TOTAL 3 HOURS, 6 MIN.**

*This Champagne cocktail is a perfect way to start off a holiday brunch; bourbon and ginger liqueur provide a warming lift to the bubbly.*

1 cup bourbon
1 cup cranberry juice
¼ cup ginger liqueur
½ tsp. orange bitters
Orange twists, cranberries (optional)
2 (750-milliliter) bottles chilled Champagne or sparkling wine

**1.** Stir together bourbon, cranberry juice, ginger liqueur, and orange bitters in a pitcher; cover and chill 3 hours.
**2.** Pour 3 Tbsp. bourbon mixture into each of 12 Champagne flutes. Place 1 orange twist and cranberries in each flute, if desired. Pour ⅓ cup Champagne into each flute.

# CLASSIC MINT JULEP

**MAKES 1 SERVING**
**HANDS-ON 10 MIN.  TOTAL 10 MIN.**

*Leftover simple syrup keeps in the refrigerator about one week and perfectly sweetens iced tea.*

3 mint leaves
1 Tbsp. Mint Simple Syrup
Crushed ice
1½ to 2 Tbsp. bourbon
1 (4-inch) cocktail straw
1 fresh mint sprig

**1.** Muddle first 2 ingredients against sides of a chilled julep cup to release flavors. Pack cup tightly with crushed ice; pour bourbon over ice. Insert straw, place mint sprig directly next to straw, and serve immediately.

## MINT SIMPLE SYRUP

**MAKES 2 CUPS  HANDS-ON 15 MIN.**
**TOTAL 15 MIN., PLUS 1 DAY FOR CHILLING**

1 cup sugar
10 to 12 fresh mint sprigs

**1.** Bring sugar and 1 cup water to a boil in a medium saucepan. Boil, stirring often, 5 minutes or until sugar dissolves. Remove from heat; add mint, and cool completely. Pour into a glass jar; cover and chill 24 hours. Remove and discard mint.

# OYSTER FRITTERS

**MAKES 10 SERVINGS**
**HANDS-ON 26 MIN.  TOTAL 1 HOUR, 26 MIN.**

*Simple fried oysters get a hit of extra flavor from beer-spiked batter and Jalapeño-Cilantro Aïoli.*

1¾ cups all-purpose flour, divided
⅓ cup plain yellow cornmeal
2 tsp. lemon zest
1 tsp. table salt, divided
¼ tsp. ground red pepper
1 cup lager beer
1 large egg
Peanut oil
¼ tsp. freshly ground black pepper
2 pt. fresh select oysters, drained
Jalapeño-Cilantro Aïoli

**1.** Whisk together ¾ cup flour, cornmeal, lemon zest, ½ tsp. salt, and ground red pepper in a large bowl. Whisk together beer and egg. Whisk beer mixture into flour mixture until blended. Cover and let stand at room temperature 1 hour.
**2.** Pour oil to depth of 2 inches into a large Dutch oven; heat to 350°.
**3.** Meanwhile, combine remaining 1 cup flour, remaining ½ tsp. salt, and black pepper in a shallow dish. Dip oysters into seasoned flour, then dip each oyster in beer batter, allowing excess batter to drip off.
**4.** Gently lower oysters into hot oil (to prevent oysters from sticking to Dutch oven). Fry oysters, in 6 batches, 2 minutes or until golden brown. Drain on a wire rack in a jelly-roll pan over paper towels. Serve hot with Jalapeño-Cilantro Aïoli.

## JALAPEÑO-CILANTRO AÏOLI

**MAKES 1 CUP**
**HANDS-ON 5 MIN.  TOTAL 5 MIN.**

1 cup mayonnaise
1 tsp. lemon zest
1 tsp. fresh lemon juice
1 Tbsp. minced pickled sliced jalapeño peppers
2 Tbsp. chopped fresh cilantro

**1.** Stir together all ingredients in a small bowl. Cover and refrigerate until ready to serve.

Kentucky Winter Champagne Cocktail, Oyster Fritters, and Jalapeño-Cilantro Aïoli

Hot Brown Eggs Benedict
Roasted Asparagus
with Shaved Parmesan

# HOT BROWN EGGS BENEDICT

**MAKES 12 SERVINGS**
**HANDS-ON 25 MIN. TOTAL 25 MIN.**

*This dish is the breakfast version of the traditional hot brown sandwich; it features fried eggs, crumbled bacon, roasted turkey breast, and a thick, creamy sauce spooned over the top.*

½ cup butter
½ cup all-purpose flour
5 cups milk
1 cup freshly grated Pecorino Romano cheese
1 tsp. table salt
½ tsp. freshly ground black pepper
12 bacon slices
12 large eggs
12 Texas toast bread slices, toasted
4 plum tomatoes, sliced
2 lb. sliced roasted turkey breast
Garnish: chopped chives

**1.** Melt butter in a heavy saucepan over low heat; whisk in flour until smooth. Cook 1 minute, whisking constantly. Gradually whisk in milk; cook over medium heat, whisking constantly, until mixture is thickened and bubbly. Stir in cheese, salt, and pepper. Remove from heat; keep warm.

**2.** Meanwhile, cook bacon in a large nonstick skillet over medium-high heat 6 to 8 minutes or until crisp; remove bacon, and drain on paper towels, reserving 2 Tbsp. drippings in skillet. Set aside bacon.

**3.** Gently break 3 eggs into bacon drippings in hot skillet. Cook 2 to 3 minutes on each side or to desired degree of doneness. Repeat with remaining eggs.

**4.** Place 1 slice of bread on each of 12 plates; top evenly with tomato slices, turkey, and egg. Spoon sauce over tops of eggs; top with reserved bacon.

# KENTUCKY-STYLE SMOKED LEG OF LAMB

**MAKES 10 SERVINGS**
**HANDS-ON 20 MIN. TOTAL 15 HOURS**

*Kentucky folk enjoy their smoked lamb and mutton all year long on festive occasions. This lamb is slathered in a fragrant rub and left to marinate in the refrigerator for 12 hours before being smoked with hickory or cherrywood.*

1 small onion, quartered
8 garlic cloves
2 Tbsp. smoked paprika
2 Tbsp. chopped fresh rosemary
1 Tbsp. fennel seeds, crushed
1 Tbsp. lemon zest
2 tsp. kosher salt
2 tsp. freshly ground black pepper
5 Tbsp. olive oil
2 (4-lb.) boneless leg of lamb roasts
4 cups hickory or cherrywood chips

**1.** Process first 8 ingredients in a food processor until smooth, stopping to scrape down sides as needed. With processor running, gradually add oil in a slow, steady stream. Rub paste mixture over lamb. Place lamb in a large shallow dish or 2 large zip-top plastic freezer bags. Cover or seal, and chill 12 hours.

**2.** Remove lamb from refrigerator; let stand at room temperature 30 minutes. Meanwhile, soak wood chips in water 30 minutes. Light 1 side of grill, heating to 250° to 300° (low heat); leave other side unlit. Spread wood chips on a large sheet of heavy-duty aluminum foil; fold edges to seal. Poke several holes in top of pouch with a fork. Place pouch directly on lit side of grill; cover with grill lid.

**3.** Place lamb, skin side up, over unlit side, and grill, covered with grill lid, 30 minutes. Turn lamb; grill, covered with grill lid, 2 more hours or until a meat thermometer inserted in thickest portion registers 140° or until desired degree of doneness. Transfer lamb to a serving platter; cover with aluminum foil. Let stand 10 minutes before slicing.

## ROASTED ASPARAGUS WITH SHAVED PARMESAN

**MAKES 12 SERVINGS**
**HANDS-ON 13 MIN. TOTAL 23 MIN.**

*The delicate flavor of asparagus is complemented by the sharper, salty Parmesan cheese in this winning side dish.* *(Pictured on page 14)*

4 lb. thin fresh asparagus
6 Tbsp. olive oil
4 Tbsp. dry vermouth or white wine
2 Tbsp. fresh lemon juice
4 tsp. minced garlic
1½ tsp. table salt
1 tsp. freshly ground black pepper
Garnish: shaved Parmesan

**1.** Preheat oven to 450°. Snap off, and discard tough ends of asparagus. Place on a lightly greased jelly-roll pan. Whisk together olive oil and next 5 ingredients; drizzle over asparagus, tossing to coat.

**2.** Bake at 450° for 10 minutes or until crisp-tender. Transfer to a serving platter.

## WINTER FRUIT COMPOTE

**MAKES 12 SERVINGS**
**HANDS-ON 40 MIN. TOTAL 3 HOURS, 30 MIN.**

1½ cups sugar
3 cups Champagne or sparkling wine
6 Ruby Red grapefruit, peeled and sectioned
6 oranges, peeled and sectioned
Garnish: pomegranate seeds

**1.** Cook sugar in a small saucepan over medium heat, tilting pan occasionally, 10 minutes or until caramel colored. Remove from heat, and gradually pour Champagne over sugar (mixture will bubble and seize). Let stand 5 minutes.

**2.** Cook mixture over medium-low heat, stirring occasionally, 15 minutes or until sugar is dissolved (mixture will be syrupy). Remove from heat, and cool 30 minutes.

**3.** Combine grapefruit and orange sections in a bowl. Pour Champagne mixture over fruit. Cover and chill 2 to 24 hours.

## DECADENT CHOCOLATE-BOURBON PECAN PIE

**MAKES 8 TO 10 SERVINGS**
**HANDS-ON 18 MIN. TOTAL 4 HOURS, 18 MIN.**

*This deep-dish rendition of the famous "Derby Pie" is loaded with luscious chocolate, bourbon, and pecans for a decadent Bluegrass dessert.*

1 (14.1-oz.) package refrigerated piecrusts
1½ cups light corn syrup
¾ cup granulated sugar
¾ cup firmly packed brown sugar
½ cup butter
5 large eggs
6 Tbsp. bourbon
2 tsp. vanilla extract
¾ tsp. table salt
⅔ cup semisweet chocolate morsels
⅔ cup milk chocolate morsels
1¼ cups chopped pecans
Garnishes: mint sprig, whipped cream, chopped pecans, shaved chocolate

**1.** Preheat oven to 325°. Unroll piecrusts; stack on a lightly greased surface. Roll stacked piecrusts into a 14-inch circle. Fit piecrust into a 9-inch deep-dish pie plate according to package directions; fold edges under, and crimp.

**2.** Combine corn syrup and next 3 ingredients in a medium saucepan. Cook 6 to 8 minutes over medium heat, stirring constantly, or until butter is melted and sugar is dissolved. Remove from heat.

**3.** Whisk together eggs and next 3 ingredients. Gradually pour sugar mixture into egg mixture, whisking constantly. Stir in semisweet chocolate morsels and next 2 ingredients. Pour filling into prepared piecrust.

**4.** Bake at 325° for 1 hour or until set, shielding crust with aluminum foil, if necessary, to prevent excessive browning; cool completely on a wire rack (about 3 hours).

Decadent Chocolate-Bourbon Pecan Pie

# SORGHUM-APPLE STACK CAKE

**MAKES 20 SERVINGS**
**HANDS-ON 53 MIN. TOTAL 3 HOURS, 33 MIN.**

*Appalachian stack cakes are traditionally several layers of dry, cookie-like cakes sandwiched with an apple butter filling made from dried apples. Wrapped and left to stand for a couple of days, the cake layers absorb the moisture and flavor from the apple filling. This version is updated to accommodate modern preferences for a moist, tender layer cake without the need for two days of standing time.*

FILLING
4½ cups chopped dried apples
4½ cups apple cider
6 Tbsp. granulated sugar
½ tsp. ground cinnamon

CAKE
1½ cups butter, softened
1¾ cups firmly packed light brown sugar
3 large eggs
¾ cup sorghum syrup
4½ cups all-purpose flour
1½ tsp. baking soda
1½ tsp. ground cinnamon
1 tsp. ground ginger
¾ tsp. table salt
⅜ tsp. ground cloves
1½ cups buttermilk
2½ cups whipping cream
⅓ cup powdered sugar
Garnish: ground cinnamon

**1.** Prepare Filling: Bring apples and apple cider to a boil in a Dutch oven over medium-high heat; reduce heat to medium-low, and simmer 25 minutes or until apples are slightly softened and about two-thirds of liquid has been absorbed. Add sugar and cinnamon; simmer 10 minutes or until apples are very soft and liquid is syrupy. Remove from heat, and cool completely (about 1 hour). Process half of apple mixture in a food processor until smooth, stopping to scrape down sides as needed. Stir pureed apples into remaining apple mixture.
**2.** Prepare Cake: Preheat oven to 350°. Beat butter at medium speed with an electric mixer until creamy; gradually add brown sugar, beating until light and fluffy. Add eggs, 1 at a time, beating just until blended after each addition. Beat in sorghum syrup.
**3.** Combine flour and next 5 ingredients; add to butter mixture alternately with buttermilk, beginning and ending with flour mixture. Beat at low speed just until blended after each addition. Pour batter into 3 greased and floured 9-inch round cake pans.
**4.** Bake at 350° for 30 minutes or until a wooden pick inserted in center comes out clean. Cool in pans on wire racks 10 minutes; remove from pans to wire racks, and cool completely (about 1 hour). Cut each cake layer in half horizontally.
**5.** Beat whipping cream at medium speed with an electric mixer until foamy; gradually add powdered sugar, beating until soft peaks form.
**6.** Place 1 cake layer on a serving plate; spread 1 cup apple filling over top of cake. Place another cake layer on top of apple filling; spread 1½ cups whipped cream over top of cake. Repeat process twice ending with whipped cream. Dollop remaining filling onto center of cake, if desired.

**HOLIDAY HINTS**

## Tips for Foolproof Cakes

Follow these tips to avoid common mistakes when preparing a cake from scratch.

**If your cake falls,** it could be because your oven was not hot enough or you did not bake the cake long enough, the batter was undermixed, or too much baking powder, baking soda, liquid, or sugar was used. To avoid this, try not opening the oven door while baking and being very accurate with measuring your ingredients.

**If your cake peaks in the center,** your oven may have been too hot at the start of baking, or you could have used too much flour and not enough liquid. Again, be precise in your measurements to avoid this common mistake.

**If your cake cracks and falls apart,** try not removing it from the pan too soon. Also, it could be a result of too much shortening, baking powder, baking soda, or sugar.

1

## RINGS OF ROSES

A mass of red roses arranged on a trio of cake stands makes a lasting impression. The three dozen blooms last a week or more when placed in water-filled florist vials that are artfully camouflaged.

# RUN FOR THE ROSES

Make the traditional flower of the Kentucky Derby the centerpiece of your Christmas decor.

2

## AT YOUR SERVICE

Serve up a tray of tightly packed red and 'super green' roses, a variety with ruffled petals and a Granny Smith apple hue. This low centerpiece is ideal for conversation.

3

## GIDDY UP!

No Derby-inspired gathering would be complete without a Thoroughbred or two, and these black beauties are a fitting touch.

4

## BERRIES AND BLOOMS

A conical floral foam base provides the structure for this statement centerpiece made from more roses, red ranunculus, creamy hydrangea blossoms, and red and green hypericum berries.

# PATTERN PLAY

Create a holiday color scheme with a twist and repeat it in a variety of patterns.

1

## LIKE A DIAMOND

Leather lacing and diamond-shaped felt cutouts in red and green embellish a basic burlap wreath form, creating a classic argyle pattern. Mercury glass ornaments add sparkle.

## MIX & MATCH

Choose multiple patterns—Scotch plaid, tartan, and windowpane check—in traditional holiday red and green to add texture and interest to your decor. A bowl of plaid ornaments lends a bright spot to the table.

## SPECIAL TOUCHES

Braided leather cord secures evergreen sprigs and holly berries to linen napkins, giving the sideboard or dining table an added dose of holiday style.

4

## DECKED IN DERBY

Equestrian tack, a velvet riding cap, and an engraved silver trophy-turned-vase grace the entry hall. The banister takes the place of a mantelpiece for these stockings trimmed with ribbon, beaded garland, and greenery.

# Boxing Day Lunch

*Based on the day-after-Christmas tradition in Great Britain, celebrate Boxing Day with a menu that incorporates holiday leftovers.*

THE MENU
Boxing Day Lunch
serves 8
TURKEY POTATO SOUP
WINTER VEGETABLE SOUP
GLAZED HAM SANDWICH
WITH JEZEBEL SAUCE
CLEMENTINE, DATE,
AND STILTON SALAD
HAM AND SWEET POTATO TART
SPICED EGGNOG BREAD
PUDDING

**Turkey Potato Soup**

# TURKEY POTATO SOUP

**MAKES 6 TO 8 SERVINGS**
**HANDS-ON 13 MIN. TOTAL 23 MIN.**

*Chop up your leftover turkey or chicken and baked potatoes to create a hearty, satisfying soup. If you don't have leftover baked potatoes, microwave two potatoes to use in soup.*

5 bacon slices
1 medium-size sweet onion, chopped
2 carrots, chopped
3 garlic cloves, chopped
7 cups chicken broth or turkey broth
2 baked potatoes, chopped
3 cups shredded turkey or chicken
1 (15-oz.) can great Northern beans, drained and rinsed
2 tsp. ground coriander
½ tsp. table salt
½ tsp. dried crushed red pepper
¼ tsp. freshly ground black pepper
Garnish: chopped fresh cilantro or parsley

**1.** Cook bacon in a large skillet over medium-high heat 5 to 7 minutes or until crisp; remove bacon, and drain on paper towels, reserving 2 Tbsp. drippings in skillet. Crumble bacon.
**2.** Sauté onion, carrots, and garlic in hot drippings 6 minutes or until tender. Stir in broth and next 7 ingredients. Bring to a boil, reduce heat, and simmer 10 minutes. Stir in crumbled bacon.

# WINTER VEGETABLE SOUP

**MAKES 8 SERVINGS**
**HANDS-ON 16 MIN. TOTAL 26 MIN.**

*Don't throw out your leftover mashed potatoes and roasted vegetables; toss them into this simple, creamy soup and have them for lunch!*

1 cup coarsely chopped parsnips
1 cup coarsely chopped carrots
1 cup coarsely chopped turnips
1 cup halved Brussels sprouts
3 Tbsp. olive oil, divided
1 tsp. table salt, divided
¾ tsp. freshly ground black pepper, divided
1 medium onion, diced
3 garlic cloves, minced
2 cups mashed potatoes
4 cups chicken broth
½ tsp. dried sage
1 cup whipping cream

**1.** Preheat oven to 400°. Combine parsnips, carrots, turnips, Brussels sprouts, 2 Tbsp. olive oil, ½ tsp. salt, and ¼ tsp. pepper on a lightly greased rimmed baking sheet. Bake at 400° for 10 to 15 minutes or until vegetables are browned and tender, stirring occasionally.
**2.** Meanwhile, heat remaining 1 Tbsp. olive oil in a large Dutch oven over medium-high heat; add onion, and sauté 6 minutes or until tender. Add garlic, and sauté 1 minute. Stir in roasted vegetables, mashed potatoes, broth, sage, remaining ½ tsp salt, and ½ tsp. pepper. Bring to a boil, reduce heat, and simmer 10 minutes.
**3.** Process mixture with a handheld blender or in batches in a blender until smooth. Return soup to Dutch oven; stir in cream. Cook over medium heat 3 minutes or until thoroughly heated.

## GLAZED HAM SANDWICH WITH JEZEBEL SAUCE

**MAKES 8 SERVINGS**
**HANDS-ON 12 MIN. TOTAL 22 MIN.**

*Choose the level of heat you desire when selecting your horseradish; it varies by brand.*

2 Tbsp. prepared horseradish, drained
2 Tbsp. dry mustard
½ cup pineapple preserves
½ cup apple jelly
1 tsp. freshly ground black pepper
1 cup mayonnaise
16 slices seeded multigrain bread, toasted
1 lb. Ginger-Peach Glazed Ham (page 126), cut into 8 thin slices
16 thin slices Havarti cheese
2 cups arugula

**1.** Combine first 5 ingredients in a small saucepan over medium heat; cook 4 minutes or until preserves and jelly are melted. Remove from heat; cool (about 10 minutes).
**2.** Spread 2 Tbsp. mayonnaise and 2 Tbsp. jezebel sauce on 8 slices of bread. Top each with 2 ham slices, 2 cheese slices, and ¼ cup arugula. Spread 1 Tbsp. jezebel sauce on remaining 8 bread slices, and place over arugula. Cut each sandwich in half.

## CLEMENTINE, DATE, AND STILTON SALAD

**MAKES 8 SERVINGS**
**HANDS-ON 12 MIN. TOTAL 12 MIN.**

*This salad makes the most of winter's clementines, moist Medjool dates, Stilton cheese, and candied walnuts tossed with colorful mixed baby greens. Seconds anyone?*

6 clementines
2 Tbsp. white balsamic vinegar
2 tsp. honey
¼ cup canola oil
¼ tsp. table salt
¼ tsp. freshly ground black pepper
8 cups spring greens mix
¾ cup chopped dried Medjool dates
¾ cup crumbled Stilton cheese
½ cup coarsely chopped candied walnuts

**1.** Grate zest from 2 clementines to equal 1 tsp. Cut 2 clementines in half; squeeze juice from clementines into a measuring cup to equal 2 Tbsp. Peel and slice remaining 4 clementines.
**2.** Whisk together clementine juice, clementine zest, white balsamic vinegar, and next 4 ingredients.
**3.** Arrange salad greens on a serving platter. Top greens with sliced clementines, dates, Stilton cheese, and candied walnuts. Drizzle with vinaigrette, or serve on the side.

## HAM AND SWEET POTATO TART

**MAKES 8 SERVINGS**
**HANDS-ON 30 MIN. TOTAL 1 HOUR, 45 MIN.**

*If you have any leftover green beans or sweet potatoes from your holiday meal, use them in this recipe. They make it easy to whip together a homemade tart with the addition of cheese and other on-hand staples.*

½ (14.1-oz.) package refrigerated piecrusts
1 cup cubed peeled sweet potato
1 cup (1-inch slices) fresh green beans
2 Tbsp. butter
2 medium leeks, sliced
2 cups chopped fully cooked ham
3 large eggs
1 cup heavy cream
1 cup (4 oz.) shredded fontina cheese
¼ tsp. table salt
¼ tsp. freshly ground black pepper

**1.** Preheat oven to 425°. Roll piecrust into a 13-inch circle. Fit into a 10-inch deep-dish pie plate. Line pastry with aluminum foil, and fill with pie weights or dried beans.
**2.** Bake at 425° for 7 minutes. Remove weights and foil, and bake 3 more minutes or until bottom is golden brown. Reduce oven temperature to 350°.
**3.** Cook sweet potatoes in boiling water to cover 8 minutes; add green beans, and cook 6 minutes. Drain and set aside.
**4.** Melt butter in a medium skillet over medium heat; add leeks, and sauté 4 minutes or until tender. Add ham, sweet potatoes, and green beans; sauté 3 minutes. Remove from heat. Cool 10 minutes.
**5.** Combine eggs and cream in a large bowl. Add leek mixture, fontina cheese, salt, and pepper. Pour into prepared piecrust.
**6.** Bake at 350° for 45 minutes or until center is set, shielding edges with aluminum foil after 30 minutes to prevent excessive browning, if necessary. Remove from oven, and let stand 20 minutes before serving.

Clementine, Date, and Stilton Salad

Glazed Ham Sandwich with Jezebel Sauce

# SPICED EGGNOG BREAD PUDDING

**MAKES 12 SERVINGS**
**HANDS-ON 10 MIN. TOTAL 1 HOUR, 25 MIN.**

*This bourbon-spiked eggnog bread pudding makes good use of leftover bread or rolls and eggnog from the holiday festivities.*

1 (16-oz.) day-old French bread loaf, cut into 1-inch cubes (12 cups)
4 large eggs
½ cup granulated sugar
½ cup bourbon, divided
3½ cups eggnog
1 tsp. vanilla extract
¼ tsp. freshly grated nutmeg
¼ tsp. ground allspice
1 cup whipping cream
2 Tbsp. powdered sugar
Garnish: freshly grated nutmeg

**1.** Preheat oven to 350°. Place bread cubes in a lightly greased 13- x 9-inch baking dish or 12 individual ramekins.
**2.** Whisk together eggs, granulated sugar, ⅓ cup bourbon, and next 4 ingredients. Pour eggnog mixture over bread cubes, stirring gently. Cover and chill 30 minutes or until bread has absorbed most of egg mixture.
**3.** Bake at 350° for 45 minutes or until set.
**4.** Meanwhile, beat whipping cream and remaining bourbon until foamy; gradually add powdered sugar, beating until soft peaks form. Serve bread pudding warm with bourbon whipped cream.

# BOXED UP AND READY TO GO

Boxing Day is celebrated around the world in many ways. Most often, it's a day spent relaxing, shopping, and playing games.

1

## GAME ON

Enjoy a little relaxation time and healthy competition with a variety of board games.

2

## JARS OF JOY

Red and white elements from deconstructed holiday centerpieces are recycled in casual arrangements for the table and in posies guests can take home.

## FLAG FUN

A British Union Jack is a fitting flourish for a holiday long observed across the pond.

4

## SILVER LININGS

Adding sparkle to the bar, holiday decorations are enjoyed for a final day before they are boxed up for next year.

# Southern-style Cocktail Party

*Use classic Southern ingredients to create unexpected sips and nibbles for a glam gathering that will wow family and friends.*

THE MENU
Southern-style Cocktail Party
serves 12
HONEY BOURBON SWEET TEA
MOONSHINE KISS
MERRY BERRY CHRISTMAS, SUGAR!
POMEGRANATE MARTINI
BEEF TENDERLOIN CROSTINI
SMOKED GOUDA AND COUNTRY HAM GRITS PILLOWS
CRANBERRY CHEESE BITES
SMOKED CHICKEN BUTTERMILK BISCUIT SLIDERS
BOOZY CHERRY BURRATA (DOUBLE RECIPE)
RED VELVET-PEPPERMINT SWIRL BROWNIES
PECAN PIE COOKIES

## HONEY BOURBON SWEET TEA

**MAKES 8 SERVINGS**
**HANDS-ON 11 MIN. TOTAL 3 HOURS, 41 MIN.**

*Making homemade simple syrup is a snap and is leaps and bounds better in flavor than the store-bought variety.*

1 cup sugar
2 fresh mint sprigs
4 cups refrigerated unsweetened tea
1½ cups honey bourbon
2 cups refrigerated lemonade
Crushed ice
Garnishes: lemon slices, mint sprigs

**1.** Combine sugar and 1 cup water in a small saucepan; heat, stirring constantly, until sugar dissolves. Remove from heat; add 2 mint sprigs, and cool completely. Discard mint sprigs. Combine tea, simple syrup, bourbon, and lemonade in a large pitcher. Chill until ready to serve. Serve over crushed ice.

**NOTE:** We tested with Jim Beam Honey Bourbon and Simply Lemonade.

## MOONSHINE KISS

**MAKES 1 SERVING**
**HANDS-ON 5 MIN. TOTAL 5 MIN.**

*Made with legalized moonshine, this cocktail kiss is sure to impress. It can be multiplied and prepared ahead for a party. Store in the refrigerator until serving time.*

3 Tbsp. moonshine
3 Tbsp. bottled pear nectar
1½ Tbsp. ginger liqueur
1 tsp. fresh lemon juice
1 Tbsp. ginger simple syrup
½ cup ice cubes
Garnish: lemon peel

**1.** Combine first 5 ingredients in a cocktail shaker. Add ice cubes. Cover with lid, and shake vigorously until thoroughly chilled (about 30 seconds). Strain into a chilled stemmed glass.

## MERRY BERRY CHRISTMAS, SUGAR!

**MAKES 1 SERVING**
**HANDS-ON 5 MIN. TOTAL 5 MIN.**

5 fresh raspberries
4 fresh blueberries
2 fresh blackberries
1½ Tbsp. light agave nectar
5 fresh mint leaves
2 Tbsp. fresh lime juice
1 cup crushed ice
2 Tbsp. chilled ginger ale
Garnish: fresh raspberries

**1.** Muddle raspberries, blueberries, blackberries, agave nectar, mint leaves, and lime juice against sides of a cocktail shaker to release flavors. Stir in crushed ice and 6 Tbsp. water. Cover with lid, and shake vigorously until thoroughly chilled (7 to 10 seconds). Strain into a chilled 16-oz. glass, and top with ginger ale.

## POMEGRANATE MARTINI

**MAKES 1 SERVING**
**HANDS-ON 5 MIN. TOTAL 5 MIN.**

¼ cup orange-flavored vodka
3 Tbsp. chilled pomegranate juice
2 Tbsp. simple syrup
1 Tbsp. orange liqueur
Ice cubes
Garnish: rosemary sprig

**1.** Combine first 4 ingredients in a cocktail shaker filled with ice. Cover with lid, and shake vigorously until thoroughly chilled (about 30 seconds). Strain into a chilled martini glass.

Pomegrante
Martini
Merry Berry
Christmas, Sugar!
Moonshine Kiss
Honey Bourbon
Sweet Tea

# BEEF TENDERLOIN CROSTINI

**MAKES 3 DOZEN**
**HANDS-ON 45 MIN. TOTAL 1 HOUR, 35 MIN.**

CILANTRO SAUCE

2 tsp. cumin seeds
1½ cups firmly packed fresh cilantro leaves
⅓ cup olive oil
1 garlic clove
2 Tbsp. fresh lime juice
½ tsp. kosher salt

MANGO-RED ONION RELISH

½ cup diced red onion
1 tsp. olive oil
1 large mango, peeled and diced
¼ cup diced red bell pepper
1 jalapeño pepper, seeded and minced
1 Tbsp. Champagne vinegar

BEEF TENDERLOIN

1 lb. beef tenderloin fillets
1 Tbsp. olive oil
1 tsp. kosher salt
½ tsp. freshly ground black pepper
⅛ tsp. garlic powder
Herbed Cornbread Crostini

**1.** Prepare Cilantro Sauce: Place a small skillet over medium-high heat until hot; add cumin seeds, and cook, stirring constantly, 1 to 2 minutes or until toasted. Cool 10 minutes. Process cilantro, next 4 ingredients, 2 Tbsp. water, and toasted cumin seeds in a blender until smooth, stopping to scrape down sides as needed. Cover and chill until ready to serve.

**2.** Prepare Mango-Red Onion Relish: Sauté onion in 1 tsp. hot olive oil in a small skillet over medium-high heat 6 to 8 minutes or until onion is tender. Transfer to a medium bowl, and stir in mango, next 3 ingredients, and table salt and freshly ground black pepper to taste.

**3.** Prepare Beef Tenderloin: Rub steaks with 1 Tbsp. olive oil. Sprinkle with 1 tsp. salt and next 2 ingredients. Place a grill pan over medium-high heat until hot; cook steaks 8 minutes on each side or to desired degree of doneness. Let stand 5 minutes. Thinly slice steak.

**4.** Top flat sides of Herbed Cornbread Crostini with relish and steak; drizzle with Cilantro Sauce.

## HERBED CORNBREAD CROSTINI

**MAKES 3 DOZEN**
**HANDS-ON 15 MIN. TOTAL 23 MIN.**

Preheat oven to 450°. Stir together 2 cups self-rising white cornmeal mix and 2 Tbsp. sugar in a large bowl; make a well in center of mixture. Whisk together 2 large eggs; ½ cup sour cream; ½ cup buttermilk; and ½ cup butter, melted, in a medium bowl. Add to cornmeal mixture, stirring just until dry ingredients are moistened. Fold in 2 Tbsp. each chopped fresh chives and parsley. Spoon batter into 3 lightly greased 12-cup muffin pans (about 1 Tbsp. per cup), spreading batter to cover bottoms of cups. Bake 8 minutes or until set. Immediately remove from pans to wire racks. Serve warm.

**HOLIDAY HINTS**

### Freeze Ahead

**Get a jump-start** on the busy holiday season by making and freezing the Herbed Cornbread Crostini ahead. Prepare the crostini as directed, and cool completely. Freeze in zip-top plastic freezer bags up to one month, if desired. To serve, arrange desired number of cornbread rounds on a baking sheet, and bake at 350° for 5 to 6 minutes or until thoroughly heated.

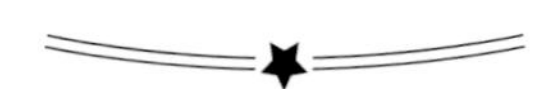

Cranberry Cheese Bites

Smoked Gouda and Country Ham Grits Pillows

# SMOKED GOUDA AND COUNTRY HAM GRITS PILLOWS

**MAKES 12 TO 14 SERVINGS**
**HANDS-ON 47 MIN. TOTAL 3 HOURS, 17 MIN.**

*These cheesy, salty grits pillows can be served with any number of savory toppings such as chutneys, compotes, or relishes.*

1 Tbsp. butter
1 cup (4 oz.) finely chopped country ham
3 Tbsp. finely chopped shallot
½ tsp. chopped fresh thyme
1 cup heavy cream
2 tsp. table salt
2½ cups uncooked stone-ground grits
1 cup (4 oz.) shredded smoked Gouda cheese
½ tsp. freshly ground black pepper
5 large eggs
Canola oil
3 cups panko (Japanese breadcrumbs)

**1.** Melt butter in a large Dutch oven over medium-high heat. Add country ham; cook 4 minutes or until almost crisp. Add shallots and thyme; cook 3 minutes. Add 9 cups water, cream, and salt. Bring mixture to a boil. Gradually whisk in grits; return to a boil. Reduce heat to medium-low; cook, whisking often, 25 minutes or until thickened. Remove from heat; stir in cheese, pepper, and 3 eggs, whisking until well blended.
**2.** Spread grits in a lightly greased jelly-roll pan. Cool 30 minutes; cover and chill 2 hours or overnight.
**3.** Pour oil to depth of 2 inches into a Dutch oven; heat to 340°.
**4.** Cut chilled grits into 35 (2-inch) circles.
**5.** Whisk together remaining 2 eggs and 2 Tbsp. water in a small bowl. Place panko in a shallow dish or pie plate. Dredge grits cakes in egg mixture, and dredge in panko. Cook grits cakes, in batches, in hot oil 2 minutes or until golden brown. Drain on paper towels.

# CRANBERRY CHEESE BITES

**MAKES 30 SERVINGS**
**HANDS-ON 1 HOUR, 13 MIN. TOTAL 1 HOUR, 58 MIN.**

*You can prepare the cranberry jelly ahead of time to make prep even faster on the day you plan to serve these cheesy bites. Use any leftover jelly to serve with turkey.*

1 cup fresh or frozen cranberries, thawed
1 (10.5-oz.) jar red pepper jelly
¼ cup sugar
¼ tsp. dried crushed red pepper
1 tsp. chopped fresh rosemary
2 (2.1-oz.) packages frozen mini-phyllo pastry shells, thawed
1 (8-oz.) package Camembert cheese, cut into ½-inch cubes
½ cup toasted pecan halves
Garnish: small rosemary sprigs

**1.** Bring cranberries, jelly, sugar, ¼ cup water, and crushed red pepper to a boil in a large saucepan over medium heat, stirring often. Reduce heat, and simmer, stirring often, 10 to 15 minutes or until cranberry skins begin to split and mixture begins to thicken. Remove from heat, and stir in chopped rosemary. Cool completely (about 45 minutes).
**2.** Preheat oven to 375°. Place phyllo shells on a lightly greased baking sheet; place 1 cheese cube in each shell. Bake at 375° for 5 minutes or until cheese is melted. Top melted cheese with ½ tsp. jelly mixture and 1 pecan half. Serve immediately.

# SMOKED CHICKEN BUTTERMILK BISCUIT SLIDERS

**MAKES 16 SERVINGS**
**HANDS-ON 35 MIN. TOTAL 1 HOUR**

*Moist, tender mini buttermilk chive biscuits are filled with smoked chicken and creamy pickled okra-studded slaw for a filling appetizer.*

¼ cup sliced red onion
½ cup cold butter, cut into pieces
2½ cups self-rising soft-wheat flour
2 Tbsp. chopped fresh chives
1 cup buttermilk
Self-rising soft-wheat flour
Parchment paper
2 Tbsp. butter, melted
2½ cups shredded coleslaw mix
½ cup sliced pickled okra
½ cup white barbecue sauce
1 lb. smoked chicken, shredded and coarsely chopped

**1.** Place oven rack in top third of oven. Preheat oven to 450°. Place onion in a small bowl; cover with cold water, and set aside.

**2.** Sprinkle 2 Tbsp. cold butter over flour, and toss. Cut remaining cold butter into flour with a pastry blender or fork until mixture resembles small peas and dough is crumbly. Cover and chill 10 minutes. Stir in chives. Add buttermilk, stirring just until dry ingredients are moistened.

**3.** Turn dough out onto a lightly floured surface, and knead 3 or 4 times, gradually adding additional self-rising flour as needed. With floured hands, pat dough into a ¾-inch-thick rectangle (about 9 x 5 inches); dust top with flour. Fold dough over itself in 3 sections, starting with short end (as if folding a letter-size piece of paper). Repeat 2 more times, beginning with patting dough into a rectangle.

**4.** Pat dough to ½-inch thickness. Cut with a 1¾-inch round cutter, and place, side by side, on a parchment paper-lined or lightly greased jelly-roll pan. (Dough rounds should touch.)

**5.** Bake at 450° for 15 minutes or until lightly browned. Remove from oven; brush with 2 Tbsp. melted butter.

**6.** Meanwhile, drain onion from water. Combine coleslaw mix, okra, red onion, and white barbecue sauce, tossing to coat.

**7.** Split biscuits. Top bottom half of biscuits evenly with smoked chicken and slaw. Cover with top half of biscuits. Serve immediately.

# BOOZY CHERRY BURRATA

**MAKES 6 TO 8 SERVINGS**
**HANDS-ON 13 MIN. TOTAL 13 HOURS, 13 MIN.**

*Burrata is made from the scraps of mozzarella cheese with the addition of added cream. The outside of each pouch is solid mozzarella, while the inside contains more oozy mozzarella and cream.*

1 (8-oz.) package fresh Burrata cheese
½ cup brandy
½ cup dried cherries
1 Tbsp. sorghum syrup
¼ tsp. chopped fresh rosemary
¼ cup toasted slivered almonds
6 frozen phyllo sheets, thawed
¼ cup butter, melted
Toasted French bread slices and apple slices

**1.** Unwrap Burrata; gently pat dry. Wrap Burrata in several layers of plastic wrap to preserve the "ball" shape. Freeze 12 hours or until completely frozen.

**2.** Bring brandy to a boil in a small saucepan. Remove from heat; add cherries. Let stand 20 minutes; drain, discarding brandy. Chop cherries; place in a small bowl. Stir in sorghum syrup, rosemary, and almonds.

**3.** Preheat oven to 400°. Place 1 phyllo sheet on a flat work surface. (Keep remaining phyllo covered with a damp towel to prevent drying out.) Brush with butter. Repeat with remaining phyllo and butter, overlapping each phyllo sheet over the previous sheet. Spoon cherry mixture in center of phyllo. Unwrap Burrata, and place on cherry mixture. Wrap phyllo around Burrata, pressing to seal tightly, and place on an aluminum foil-lined baking sheet coated with cooking spray, folded side down. Brush with remaining butter.

**4.** Bake at 400° for 40 minutes or until phyllo is golden brown. Remove from oven. Serve immediately with bread and apple slices.

**Smoked Chicken Buttermilk Biscuit Sliders**

Pecan Pie Cookies

Red Velvet-Peppermint
Swirl Brownies

## RED VELVET-PEPPERMINT SWIRL BROWNIES

**MAKES ABOUT 2 DOZEN**
**HANDS-ON 20 MIN. TOTAL 1 HOUR, 50 MIN.**

- 1 (4-oz.) bittersweet chocolate baking bar, chopped
- ¾ cup butter
- 2¼ cups sugar, divided
- 4 large eggs
- 1 (1-oz.) bottle red liquid food coloring
- ¼ tsp. peppermint extract
- 2 tsp. vanilla extract, divided
- 1½ cups all-purpose flour
- ⅛ tsp. table salt
- ½ (8-oz.) package cream cheese, softened
- 2 large egg whites
- 2 Tbsp. all-purpose flour

**1.** Preheat oven to 350°. Line bottom and sides of a 13- x 9-inch pan with aluminum foil, allowing 2 to 3 inches to extend over sides; lightly grease foil.

**2.** Microwave chocolate and butter in a large microwave-safe bowl at HIGH 1½ to 2 minutes or until melted and smooth, stirring at 30-second intervals. Whisk in 2 cups sugar. Add eggs, 1 at a time, whisking just until blended after each addition. Add food coloring, peppermint extract, and 1 tsp. vanilla. Gently stir in flour and salt. Pour batter into prepared pan.

**3.** Beat cream cheese and remaining ¼ cup sugar at medium speed with an electric mixer until fluffy. Add egg whites and remaining 1 tsp. vanilla, and beat until blended. Stir in 2 Tbsp. flour until smooth. Drop cream cheese mixture by heaping tablespoonfuls over batter in pan; gently swirl with a knife.

**4.** Bake at 350° for 30 to 32 minutes or until a wooden pick inserted in center comes out with a few moist crumbs. Cool completely in pan on a wire rack (about 1 hour). Lift brownies from pan, using foil sides as handles. Gently remove foil; cut brownies into squares.

## PECAN PIE COOKIES

**MAKES 2 DOZEN**
**HANDS-ON 12 MIN. TOTAL 57 MIN.**

*For pecan pie purists, the chocolate drizzle is optional.*

### COOKIE DOUGH

- ⅔ cup toasted pecan halves
- 1¼ cups butter, softened
- ¾ cup powdered sugar
- 1 tsp. vanilla extract
- 2¼ cups all-purpose flour
- ¼ tsp. table salt

### FILLING

- ¼ cup plus 2 Tbsp. firmly packed dark brown sugar
- 3 Tbsp. butter, melted
- 4½ Tbsp. light corn syrup
- 1½ tsp. vanilla extract
- ¼ tsp. table salt
- 2 large egg yolks
- 1½ cups chopped pecans
- 1 (4-oz.) bittersweet chocolate baking bar, chopped

**1.** Prepare Cookie Dough: Process pecan halves in a food processor 15 seconds or until coarsely ground. Beat butter at medium speed with an electric mixer until creamy. Gradually add powdered sugar, beating well. Beat in vanilla. Combine flour, salt, and ground pecans; gradually add to butter mixture, beating until blended.

**2.** Shape dough into 24 (1-inch) balls. Place into lightly greased mini muffin pans; press into cups. Preheat oven to 350°.

**3.** Prepare Filling: Stir together dark brown sugar and next 6 ingredients. Spoon about 1 Tbsp. filling into each muffin cup, stirring after filling each cup to blend nuts. Bake at 350° for 15 minutes or until edges are lightly browned. Cool in pans 10 minutes. Loosen edges with knife; transfer to wire racks to cool completely (about 20 minutes).

**4.** Microwave chocolate in a microwave-safe bowl at HIGH 1 to 1½ minutes or until melted, stirring at 30-second intervals. Drizzle chocolate over cookies. Let stand until chocolate is set.

# ALL IS BRIGHT!

Dusty pink and cream flowers inspire the palette for this holiday setting. Vintage Lusterware and heirloom ornaments combine with flowers, fruit, and new finds with fanciful effect.

1

## PRETTY IN PINK

A blushing Kris Kringle decked out in pink is surprisingly suited to this scene. Dusty rose ranunculus, peonies, and shimmering accents add to the whimsy.

2

## LUSH AND LOVELY

The quintessential Christmas plant, poinsettia, comes in shades of solid red and cream and marbled or speckled combinations of the two.

3

## FESTIVE FLOWER

Another holiday classic, long-lasting amaryllis come in many hues and are perfect for giving, too.

## 4
## TREETOPS GLISTEN

Simple and pretty, an assortment of glittery ornaments, antique mercury glass balls, and gifts tied with velvet ribbon make a fanciful centerpiece when arranged on a vintage tiered stand.

# Harvest & Hunt Feast

*It's game-on when you prepare a feast that revolves around fall and winter hunting season. Pumpkins, antlers, and other elements of autumn reflect the field and forest theme.*

THE MENU
Harvest & Hunt Feast
serves 6
VESPERTINE
SOUTHERN 75
SHAVED BRUSSELS SPROUTS SALAD
VENISON SADDLE WITH
RED WINE-JUNIPER REDUCTION
MUSTARD-CRUSTED WILD BOAR RACK
WITH BOURBON JUS
ROASTED ROOT VEGETABLES
CORNBREAD SAUSAGE DRESSING
MUSHROOM AND PARMESAN
BREAD PUDDING
BOURBON-APPLE STICKY
TOFFEE PUDDING

# VESPERTINE

**MAKES 1 SERVING**
**HANDS-ON 3 MIN.  TOTAL 3 MIN.**

*The perfect libation for dusk, this Southern spin on a Manhattan is made with Punt e Mes sweet vermouth and garnished with an orange slice.*

¼ cup rye whiskey
2 Tbsp. sweet vermouth
1 Tbsp. artichoke-flavored bitters
⅛ tsp. orange bitters
Ice cubes
Garnish: orange slice

**1.** Combine first 4 ingredients in a cocktail shaker; add ½ cup ice cubes. Cover with lid, and shake vigorously until thoroughly chilled (about 30 seconds). Strain into an ice-filled glass.

**NOTE:** We tested with Sazerac Rye Whiskey, Cynar Bitters, and Carpano Punt e Mes Sweet Vermouth.

# FLOURISHES FOR FALL FEASTS

Hunting camp meets late season harvest to create a pretty tableau that bridges autumn and winter. Combining woodsy elements, menswear fabrics, slubby linen, and metallic accents lends rustic luxury that is anything but fussy. Creamy Lumina pumpkins, antlers, feathers, and loose arrangements of flowers and prairie grasses are ways to bring the outdoors in with an approachable casualness. Creating multiple vignettes on the dining table, sideboard, and bar adds interest wherever guests gather.

# SOUTHERN 75

**MAKES 8 SERVINGS**
**HANDS-ON 5 MIN. TOTAL 3 HOURS, 5 MIN.**

1 cup bourbon
½ cup lemon juice
⅓ cup powdered sugar
2 cups chilled hard cider (such as Angry Orchard)
Garnishes: apple slices, lemon curls, or rosemary sprigs

**1.** Stir together bourbon, lemon juice, and powdered sugar in a pitcher until sugar dissolves (about 30 seconds). Cover and chill 3 hours. Divide among 8 Champagne flutes; top each with ¼ cup chiled hard cider.

## Stock the Bar

Add cheer to any holiday get-together with a well-planned bar. Here are a few of our best tips.

**Signature Drink:** Serve a special concoction to fit the theme of your gathering.

**Ice Advice:** A good rule of thumb is to have anywhere between a half pound to one pound of ice per person. Buy bags of ice and store them in an ice chest on the deck, or, for smaller parties, empty the ice from your freezer's ice maker into an extra container the night before.

**Make It Pretty:** Instead of the standard white tablecloth-covered card table, go the extra mile. Place fresh arrangements on the bar table or offer wine charms.

# SHAVED BRUSSELS SPROUTS SALAD

**MAKES 16 SERVINGS**
**HANDS-ON 40 MIN. TOTAL 40 MIN.**

*The key to success with this salad is slicing the Brussels sprouts paper-thin.*

8 bacon slices
2 lemons
1½ Tbsp. honey
1½ tsp. chopped fresh thyme
¾ tsp. table salt
¼ tsp. freshly ground black pepper
6 Tbsp. olive oil
1¾ lb. Brussels sprouts, very thinly sliced (about 8½ cups)
1 small red onion, thinly sliced
1 red Anjou pear, chopped
½ cup coarsely chopped toasted walnuts
½ cup shaved Parmesan cheese

**1.** Cook bacon in a large skillet over medium-high heat 6 to 8 minutes or until crisp; remove bacon, and drain on paper towels, reserving 2 Tbsp. drippings in skillet. Crumble bacon.

**2.** Grate zest from lemons to equal 2 tsp. Cut lemons in half; squeeze juice from lemons to equal 6 Tbsp.

**3.** Whisk together lemon juice, lemon zest, honey, and next 3 ingredients. Gradually whisk in olive oil and reserved bacon drippings.

**4.** Combine Brussels sprouts, next 4 ingredients, and bacon in a large bowl. Drizzle vinaigrette over Brussels sprouts mixture, and toss to combine. Serve immediately.

Shaved Brussels Sprouts Salad

# VENISON SADDLE WITH RED WINE-JUNIPER REDUCTION

**MAKES 8 SERVINGS**
**HANDS-ON 40 MIN. TOTAL 10 HOURS**

*A bold-flavored red wine marinade doubles as a reduction for a venison tenderloin roasted to perfection.*

1 (750-milliliter) bottle dry red wine
6 garlic cloves, crushed
12 thyme sprigs
3 rosemary sprigs
1 Tbsp. juniper berries
4 bay leaves
2 tsp. black peppercorns
4 (1-lb.) venison tenderloins
Kitchen string
¾ tsp. kosher salt
1¼ tsp. freshly ground black pepper, divided
8 slices bacon
2 cups beef broth
2 tsp. cornstarch
1 Tbsp. cold water
¼ cup butter, cut up

**1.** Stir together first 7 ingredients in a large shallow dish or large zip-top plastic freezer bag; add venison, turning to coat. Cover or seal, and chill overnight, turning occasionally. Remove venison from marinade, reserving marinade. Pat venison dry.

**2.** Preheat oven to 425°. Place 2 tenderloins on a roasting pan; stack remaining 2 tenderloins on top of bottom tenderloins. Tie together with kitchen string, securing at 1½-inch intervals. Sprinkle with salt and ¾ teaspoon pepper. Arrange bacon slices horizontally over top of venison.

**3.** Bake at 425° for 15 minutes. Reduce heat to 350°, and bake 30 more minutes or until a meat thermometer inserted into thickest portion registers 140°. Remove from oven; let stand 10 minutes before slicing. Reserve drippings in pan.

**4.** Meanwhile, bring reserved marinade to a boil in a saucepan over medium-high heat, and boil 10 minutes. Pour mixture through a cheesecloth-lined wire-mesh strainer into a small saucepan, discarding solids. Stir in beef broth; bring to a boil, and cook 15 minutes or until reduced by half. Combine cornstarch and 1 Tbsp. cold water, stirring until smooth; whisk into sauce. Boil 1 minute or until thickened. Stir in reserved pan drippings. Remove from heat; stir in butter and remaining ½ tsp. pepper. Serve venison with sauce.

# MUSTARD-CRUSTED WILD BOAR RACK WITH BOURBON JUS

**MAKES 6 SERVINGS**
**HANDS-ON 25 MIN. TOTAL 8 HOURS**

*Serve this lovely roast alongside savory side dishes of creamy potatoes or grits and sautéed mushrooms for a hearty and delicious meal.*

½ cup stone-ground mustard
½ cup Dijon mustard
1½ Tbsp. balsamic vinegar
2 Tbsp. sorghum syrup
1 Tbsp. freshly ground black pepper
1 Tbsp. chopped fresh thyme
2 medium shallots, coarsely chopped
1 (3- to 4-lb.) rack of wild boar (10 ribs)
2 celery ribs, coarsely chopped
1 large onion, coarsely chopped
2 large carrots, coarsely chopped
2 Tbsp. olive oil
1 tsp. kosher salt
½ tsp. freshly ground black pepper
1 cup bourbon
¾ cup chicken stock
2 Tbsp. butter

**1.** Process first 7 ingredients in a food processor until a paste forms. Rub mixture over rack; cover loosely with plastic wrap, and refrigerate 6 hours or overnight. Let stand at room temperature 30 minutes before cooking.

**2.** Preheat oven to 425°. Combine celery, onion, carrots, oil, salt, and pepper in a roasting pan; toss well to coat. Place rack on top of vegetables in pan.

**3.** Bake at 425° for 15 minutes; reduce oven temperature to 350°, and bake 35 minutes or until a meat thermometer inserted into thickest portion registers 140° or to desired degree of doneness. Remove from oven; cover loosely with aluminum foil, and let stand 10 minutes.

**4.** Meanwhile, place roasting pan over high heat on 2 burners. Add bourbon and chicken stock to pan. Bring to a boil, reduce heat to medium, and simmer 6 minutes or until mixture is reduced by half, stirring to loosen browned bits from bottom of pan. Pour liquid through a fine wire-mesh strainer into a medium saucepan. Add butter, and whisk until melted. Cook over medium-high heat 2 to 3 minutes or until hot.

**5.** Cut rack into chops, and arrange on a serving platter. Serve with Bourbon Jus.

**Mustard-Crusted Wild Boar Rack with Bourbon Jus**

# ROASTED ROOT VEGETABLES

**MAKES 6 SERVINGS**
**HANDS-ON 30 MIN. TOTAL 1 HOUR, 45 MIN.**

*Use any 4-lb. combo of hardy root vegetables to make this simple side.*

- 1 lb. turnips
- 1 lb. rutabagas
- 1 lb. carrots
- 1 lb. parsnips
- 3 shallots, halved
- ½ cup olive oil
- 2 Tbsp. chopped fresh rosemary
- 2 tsp. kosher salt
- 1 tsp. freshly ground black pepper
- 8 garlic cloves

**1.** Preheat oven to 400°. Peel first 4 ingredients; cut into 1-inch pieces. (If carrots are small enough, leave them whole.) Toss with shallots and next 4 ingredients. Place in a single layer in a 17- x 11-inch jelly-roll pan. Bake 30 minutes, stirring halfway through. Add garlic; bake 45 more minutes or until tender, stirring at 15-minute intervals.

**NOTE:** You can prepare 4 hours ahead: Cool in pan 30 minutes or to room temperature; bake at 450° for 10 to 15 minutes or until hot.

# CORNBREAD SAUSAGE DRESSING

**MAKES 8 TO 10 SERVINGS**
**HANDS-ON 26 MIN. TOTAL 1 HOUR**

*If you don't have time to make your own cornbread, buy about 1 lb. cornbread in the bakery section of your local grocery store.*

2 (6-oz.) packages buttermilk cornbread mix
1 (1-lb.) package sage ground pork sausage
1 cup chopped onion
½ cup chopped celery
2 garlic cloves, minced
1 Tbsp. chopped fresh thyme
2 Tbsp. chopped fresh flat-leaf parsley
½ tsp. freshly ground black pepper
¼ tsp. table salt
2 to 3 cups chicken broth
1 large egg, lightly beaten

1. Preheat oven to 450°. Prepare cornbread according to package directions. Pour batter into a greased 13- x 9-inch pan.
2. Bake at 450° for 12 minutes or until golden. Remove from oven to a wire rack; cool completely. Crumble cornbread into a large bowl.
3. Reduce oven temperature to 350°. Cook sausage, onion, and celery in a large skillet over medium-high heat 13 minutes or until sausage crumbles and is no longer pink and vegetables are tender. Add garlic and thyme; cook 1 minute.
4. Add sausage mixture, parsley, pepper, and salt to cornbread. Stir in 2 cups chicken broth and egg until moistened, adding more broth, if necessary. Spoon into a lightly greased 13- x 9-inch baking dish.
5. Bake at 350° for 30 minutes or until golden brown.

# MUSHROOM AND PARMESAN BREAD PUDDING

**MAKES 12 SERVINGS**
**HANDS-ON 21 MIN. TOTAL 1 HOUR, 16 MIN.**

*Try this savory version of bread pudding for your next comfort food side dish. It pairs deliciously with most roasted meats and adapts well to most gravies.*

2 cups half-and-half
2 cups heavy cream
1 bay leaf
½ tsp. table salt, divided
½ tsp. freshly ground black pepper, divided
⅛ tsp. ground nutmeg
3 large eggs
2 large egg yolks
1 Tbsp. chopped fresh thyme leaves
3 Tbsp. olive oil
2 (3.5-oz.) packages fresh gourmet blend mushrooms
1 (8-oz.) package sliced baby portobello mushrooms
3 Tbsp. finely chopped shallot
3 large garlic cloves, finely chopped
1 (8-oz.) block Parmesan cheese, shredded and divided
12 oz. day-old French bread loaf, cut into 1-inch cubes (about 10 cups)

1. Preheat oven to 350°. Cook half-and-half, heavy cream, bay leaf, ¼ tsp. salt, ¼ tsp. pepper, and nutmeg in a medium-size heavy, nonaluminum saucepan over medium heat, stirring often, 6 to 8 minutes or just until bubbles appear; remove from heat.
2. Combine eggs, egg yolks, and thyme in a large bowl until egg yolks are thick and pale. Gradually whisk half of hot cream mixture into egg mixture, whisking constantly; gradually whisk egg mixture into remaining hot cream mixture, whisking constantly. Remove and discard bay leaf. Set aside egg mixture.
3. Meanwhile, heat olive oil in a large skillet over medium-high heat. Add mushrooms, shallot, garlic, remaining ¼ tsp. salt, and remaining ¼ tsp. pepper. Cook 6 minutes or until mushrooms are tender, stirring frequently.
4. Combine mushroom mixture, reserved egg mixture, 1½ cups Parmesan cheese, and bread cubes in a large bowl; toss well to combine. Let stand 15 minutes. Spoon mixture into a lightly greased 13- x 9-inch baking dish. Sprinkle with remaining ½ cup Parmesan cheese.
5. Place baking dish in a large shallow pan. Add hot water to pan one-third up sides of baking dish.
6. Bake, uncovered, at 350° for 40 to 45 minutes or until top is browned and custard is set.

# BOURBON-APPLE STICKY TOFFEE PUDDING

**MAKES 10 SERVINGS**
**HANDS-ON 30 MIN. TOTAL 1 HOUR**

*This rich, sticky toffee pudding, enhanced with the season's best apples and a bourbon-infused toffee sauce, will make your hunters swoon.*

5 cups heavy whipping cream, divided
1¾ cups firmly packed dark brown sugar
⅓ cup light corn syrup
6 Tbsp. bourbon, divided
1 cup chopped pitted dates
¾ tsp. baking soda
6 Tbsp. butter, softened
¾ cup granulated sugar
2 large eggs
1½ cups all-purpose flour
¼ tsp. table salt
1¾ cups finely chopped Fuji apples
1½ tsp. vanilla extract
2 Tbsp. powdered sugar
Garnish: coarse sea salt

**1.** Preheat oven to 325°. Bring 4 cups whipping cream and next 2 ingredients to a boil in a medium saucepan over medium heat, stirring frequently. Boil, stirring constantly, 13 to 15 minutes or until thickened and reduced to 4 cups. Remove from heat, and stir in ¼ cup bourbon. Pour ¼ cup toffee mixture into each of 10 (6-oz.) lightly greased ramekins. Reserve remaining toffee sauce.
**2.** Combine ⅔ cup water and dates in a small saucepan; bring to a boil. Remove from heat; stir in baking soda. Let stand 5 minutes.
**3.** Beat butter and granulated sugar at medium speed with an electric mixer about 2 to 3 minutes or until creamy. Add eggs, 1 at a time, beating just until yellow disappears.
**4.** Combine flour and salt; add to butter mixture alternately with date mixture, beginning and ending with flour mixture. Beat at low speed just until blended after each addition, stopping to scrape bowl as needed. Stir in chopped apples and vanilla. Spoon batter evenly into ramekins over toffee mixture. (Do not spread.)
**5.** Bake at 325° for 25 to 30 minutes or until a wooden pick inserted in center comes out almost clean. Cool 5 minutes.
**6.** Meanwhile, beat remaining 1 cup whipping cream and remaining 2 Tbsp. bourbon until foamy; gradually add powdered sugar, beating until soft peaks form. Serve puddings warm, drizzled with reserved toffee sauce. Dollop with whipped cream mixture.

**EXTRA TOUCH**
A rustic bark-covered wall pocket gets dressed up with a profusion of blooms. This arrangement would also look nice on the backs of the chairs.

# Global Gathering

*Surprise guests with Southern cocktail standards given international twists. Carry the theme through to the tableware and decorations by introducing global accents, textures, bright colors, and imported finds to create a rich tapestry of festive style and inspired flavor.*

THE MENU

## *Global Gathering*

*serves 10*

CRANBERRY MOJITO

PEAR-BASIL SIPPER

MANGOTINI

SPARKLING RUM PUNCH

BBQ PULLED PORK SOPES

KOREAN FRIED CHICKEN AND WAFFLES

SAVORY CORNCAKES WITH ZA'ATAR GREENS

ROASTED RED PEPPER SOUP (DOUBLE RECIPE)

TANDOORI-SEASONED FRIED PECAN OKRA

GREEK PIZZA

# WILD AND WORLDLY

Shop import stores and flea markets for artisan pieces and one-of-a-kind finds that say "happy holidays" in a surprising new way. This buck's papier mâché horns look surprisingly realistic while its climbing-rope hide is anything but.

# CHRISTMAS AROUND THE WORLD AT HOME

Handmade goods and one-of-a-kind finds from artisans around the globe add color and character perfect for an evening gathering that celebrates international flavors. Beautiful textiles and distressed wood are layered with global flourishes accumulated over years of travel to drive home the universal theme. Think "double duty" when decorating. A stack of colorful shawls by the fire are pretty and useful. Handmade beads made of thread go from necklace to striking garland. And primitive ornaments make lasting favors.

### SPECIAL DELIVERY

An old steamer trunk is a perfect perch for gifts, cocktails and nibbles, or tired feet.

## DAZZLING DISPLAY

Set out favors and good wishes on a table by the door. Trinket and message-filled paper Christmas crackers are a 19th century invention as enduring as the fortune cookie.

Cranberry Mojito

Pear-Basil Sipper

Mangotini

## CRANBERRY MOJITO

**MAKES 1 SERVING**
**HANDS-ON 5 MIN. TOTAL 5 MIN.**

3 fresh mint leaves
1 Tbsp. Cranberry Reduction
1½ tsp. fresh lime juice
Ice cubes
3 Tbsp. rum
Lemon-lime soft drink
Garnishes: fresh mint sprig, fresh cranberries

**1.** Muddle mint leaves, Cranberry Reduction, and fresh lime juice against sides of a cocktail shaker to release flavors; add ice cubes and rum. Cover with lid, and shake vigorously until thoroughly chilled (about 30 seconds). Strain into a 10-oz. glass filled with ice cubes. Top with lemon-lime soft drink. Serve immediately.

### CRANBERRY REDUCTION

**MAKES 1¼ CUPS**
**HANDS-ON 10 MIN.**
**TOTAL 2 HOURS, 5 MIN.**

2 cups cranberry juice
½ cup jellied cranberry sauce
¼ cup sugar
4 dashes of Angostura bitters
1 (3-inch) rosemary sprig

**1.** Boil first 4 ingredients in a medium saucepan over medium heat, stirring often, 4 to 5 minutes or until smooth. Reduce heat to low, and simmer, stirring occasionally, 20 minutes or until liquid is reduced by half and slightly thickened.
**2.** Add rosemary; cover and let stand 5 minutes. Discard rosemary. Cool mixture 30 minutes. Cover and chill 1 hour. Store in an airtight container in refrigerator up to 1 week.

## PEAR-BASIL SIPPER

**MAKES 1 SERVING**
**HANDS-ON 5 MIN. TOTAL 5 MIN.**

Fresh basil leaves
½ tsp. sugar
1 cup crushed ice
4 Tbsp. pear nectar
3 Tbsp. pear-flavored vodka
3 Tbsp. lemon-lime soft drink
Garnishes: fresh basil sprig, pear slice

**1.** Muddle basil leaves and sugar against sides of a cocktail shaker to release flavors. Add crushed ice, pear nectar, and pear-flavored vodka. Cover with lid, and shake vigorously until thoroughly chilled (about 30 seconds). Strain into a chilled glass, and top with lemon-lime soft drink.

## MANGOTINI

**MAKES 1 SERVING**
**HANDS-ON 10 MIN. TOTAL 10 MIN.**

Crushed ice
3 Tbsp. light rum
3 Tbsp. Alizé Gold Passion
2 Tbsp. mango juice
2 tsp. fresh lime juice
Garnish: lime twist

**1.** Place ice in a cocktail shaker. Add rum, liqueur, and juices. Cover with lid; shake vigorously until thoroughly chilled (about 30 seconds). Strain mixture into a martini glass. Serve immediately.

## SPARKLING RUM PUNCH

**MAKES ABOUT 9 CUPS**
**HANDS-ON 10 MIN.**
**TOTAL 1 HOUR, 10 MIN.**

2 cups fresh orange juice
½ cup orange liqueur
½ cup dark rum
2 (750-milliliter) bottles sparkling wine, chilled
Garnish: sliced cranberries

**1.** Stir together orange juice, orange liqueur, and rum in a bowl; cover and chill 1 hour. Pour into a large pitcher and top with chilled sparkling wine. Serve immediately.

Sparkling Rum Punch

Korean Fried Chicken
and Waffles
BBQ Pulled
Pork Sopes
Savory Corncakes
with Za'atar Greens

# BBQ PULLED PORK SOPES

**MAKES 15 SERVINGS**
**HANDS-ON 38 MIN. TOTAL 38 MIN.**

*Traditional Mexican masa "pizzas" are given a Southern accent with BBQ pulled pork.*

- 1 cup masa harina
- ¾ cup warm water
- ¼ cup vegetable oil
- ¾ lb. shredded barbecued pork without sauce, coarsely chopped
- ½ cup barbecue sauce
- ¾ cup (3 oz.) crumbled queso fresco (fresh Mexican cheese)
- ¼ cup chopped fresh cilantro
- ¼ cup chopped green onions
- 4 lime wedges

Garnish: coleslaw

**1.** Preheat oven to 200°. Combine masa harina and ¾ cup warm water in a large bowl; knead until smooth and uniform. (Dough should be moist; add more water if needed.) Divide dough into 30 equal portions; shape into ¾-inch balls. Cover dough with plastic wrap to prevent drying out.

**2.** Roll 1 dough ball into a ¼-inch-thick circle. Cover with plastic wrap. Repeat procedure with remaining dough balls.

**3.** Heat 1 Tbsp. oil in a medium skillet over medium-high heat. Cook dough in 4 batches, using 1 Tbsp. oil per batch, 1 second or until lightly browned. Lift edge of sopes with a spatula to test for doneness. Turn sopes over, and cook about 45 seconds or until golden brown. Place sopes on a wire rack in a jelly-roll pan, and keep warm in a 200° oven.

**4.** Microwave barbecued pork in a medium-size microwave-safe bowl 1 minute or until thoroughly heated. Stir in barbecue sauce.

**5.** Divide pork evenly among sopes. Sprinkle evenly with queso fresco, cilantro, and green onions. Squeeze lime wedges over sopes. Serve warm.

# KOREAN FRIED CHICKEN AND WAFFLES

**MAKES 40 SERVINGS**
**HANDS-ON 40 MIN. TOTAL 50 MIN.**

*These Asian-inspired chicken and waffles incorporate a cornstarch- and water-based dredging mixture to produce a thin, crisp crust. A homemade Korean barbecue sauce drizzled on top completes the dish and adds a hit of heat.*

Peanut or canola oil

- ½ cup all-purpose flour
- ½ cup cornstarch
- 1 tsp. baking powder
- 1 cup cold water
- 1¾ lb. skinned and boned chicken thighs, cut into 1½-inch pieces
- 1 (10.9-oz.) package frozen mini waffles
- ½ cup soy sauce
- 2 Tbsp. dark sesame oil
- ¼ cup firmly packed brown sugar
- 2 tsp. sambal oelek
- 2 tsp. grated fresh ginger

Garnish: chopped parsley

**1.** Pour oil to depth of 2 inches into a Dutch oven; heat to 350°.

**2.** Combine flour, cornstarch, and baking powder in a large bowl. Whisk in 1 cup cold water until smooth. Dip chicken in flour mixture, shaking off excess. Fry chicken, in batches, 8 minutes or until done. Drain on a wire rack over paper towels.

**3.** Cook waffles according to package directions; separate into individual waffles. Place chicken pieces on top of waffles.

**4.** Whisk together soy sauce and next 4 ingredients in a small bowl. Drizzle over chicken.

Roasted Red Pepper Soup

# SAVORY CORNCAKES WITH ZA'ATAR GREENS

**MAKES 16 SERVINGS**
**HANDS-ON 27 MIN. TOTAL 27 MIN.**

*Southern corncakes get a Middle Eastern twist with cumin and pine nuts stirred into the batter. Za'atar is a Middle Eastern herb blend made from thyme, marjoram, oregano, sesame seed, salt, and sumac, and can be found in the ethnic aisle of grocery stores.* *(Pictured on page 68)*

1⅔ cups fresh corn kernels (3 ears)
2 garlic cloves, minced
¼ cup pine nuts
2 large eggs
½ cup plain Greek yogurt
2 Tbsp. butter, melted
½ cup all-purpose flour
½ cup plain yellow cornmeal
1 tsp. table salt, divided
¾ tsp. freshly ground black pepper, divided
½ tsp. ground cumin
¼ tsp. ground red pepper
3 Tbsp. olive oil
2 Tbsp. lemon juice
1 Tbsp. za'atar
4 cups arugula, coarsely chopped
Sliced grape tomatoes

**1.** Pulse first 3 ingredients in a food processor 3 or 4 times or just until corn is coarsely chopped. Add eggs, yogurt, and butter, and pulse until combined.
**2.** Stir together flour, cornmeal, ¾ tsp. salt, ½ tsp. black pepper, cumin, and red pepper in a large bowl; add corn mixture, stirring just until moistened.
**3.** Pour 1 Tbsp. batter for each corncake onto a hot, lightly greased griddle or into a large nonstick skillet. Cook corncakes over medium-high heat 2 minutes or until tops are covered with bubbles and edges look dry and cooked; turn and cook other side 1 to 2 minutes.
**4.** Combine olive oil, lemon juice, za'atar, and remaining ¼ tsp. salt and ¼ tsp. black pepper in a small bowl, whisking until combined. Drizzle over arugula, tossing until well coated.
**5.** To serve, arrange corncakes on a platter. Divide arugula evenly over corncakes. Top with sliced tomatoes.

# ROASTED RED PEPPER SOUP

**MAKES 6 SERVINGS**
**HANDS ON 35 MIN. TOTAL 55 MIN.**

*If you serve the soup cold, stir in an extra ¼ tsp. of table salt.*

1 Tbsp. butter
1 Tbsp. olive oil
1 garlic clove, minced
1 shallot, finely chopped
1 Tbsp. tomato paste
1 (15-oz.) jar roasted red bell peppers, drained and rinsed
4 cups reduced-sodium chicken broth
¼ cup half-and-half
1 Tbsp. chopped fresh parsley
Garnishes: peppered shrimp, fresh thyme sprigs

**1.** Melt butter with oil in a large Dutch oven over medium-high heat. Add garlic and shallot, and cook, stirring constantly, 2 minutes or until vegetables are tender. Add tomato paste, and cook, stirring constantly, 1 minute. Stir in bell peppers and chicken broth; bring to a boil. Reduce heat to medium, and simmer, stirring occasionally, 5 minutes. Remove from heat; cool 10 minutes.
**2.** Process red pepper mixture, in batches, in a blender or food processor 8 to 10 seconds until smooth, stopping to scrape down sides. Return red pepper mixture to Dutch oven; stir in half-and-half and parsley, and cook over medium heat 5 minutes or until thoroughly heated. Season with table salt and freshly ground black pepper to taste.
**3.** Ladle soup into miniature cups.

# TANDOORI-SEASONED FRIED PECAN OKRA

**MAKES 10 SERVINGS**
**HANDS-ON 40 MIN. TOTAL 40 MIN.**

*Traditional fried pecan okra is given a makeover with tandoori seasoning and an Indian-spiced yogurt dipping sauce. These tasty bites of goodness are definitely not like your mama's.*

1 cup Greek yogurt
2 green chiles, seeded and chopped
4 garlic cloves, minced
2 tsp. lime juice
2 tsp. ginger paste
1 tsp. ground coriander
1 tsp. ground cumin
1 tsp. garam masala
1½ cups all-purpose flour, divided
1 cup toasted pecans
¼ cup tandoori seasoning
1 tsp. table salt
2 large eggs
1 (16-oz.) package frozen whole okra, thawed
Peanut oil

**1.** Stir together first 8 ingredients until blended.
**2.** Place ¾ cup flour in a shallow bowl. Process pecans, remaining ¾ cup flour, tandoori seasoning, and salt in a food processor until pecans are finely ground; place in a shallow bowl. Place eggs in a shallow bowl; beat well with a whisk. Dredge okra in plain flour, dip in egg, and dredge in pecan mixture, pressing gently to adhere.
**3.** Pour oil to depth of 2 inches into a Dutch oven or cast-iron skillet; heat to 350°. Fry okra, in batches, turning once, 3 minutes or until golden; drain on paper towels. Serve with yogurt sauce.

# GREEK PIZZA

**MAKES 10 SERVINGS**
**HANDS-ON 10 MIN. TOTAL 25 MIN.**

1 lb. bakery pizza crust dough
5 cups shredded romaine lettuce
½ English cucumber, sliced
1 cup grape tomatoes, halved
½ cup thinly sliced red onion
½ to ¾ cup drained kalamata olives, halved if large
⅓ cup drained pepperoncini salad peppers
¼ cup olive oil
¼ cup red wine vinegar
1 tsp. chopped fresh oregano
1 cup deli hummus
Freshly ground black pepper

**1.** Preheat oven to 450°. Pat dough to an even thickness on a lightly greased baking sheet. Bake 15 minutes or until browned and cooked through.
**2.** Meanwhile, toss romaine lettuce and next 5 ingredients in a large bowl. Whisk together olive oil, vinegar, and oregano. Drizzle over salad, gently tossing to combine.
**3.** Spread crust evenly with hummus. Arrange salad mixture over pizza. Sprinkle with pepper. Serve immediately.

## Pizza Pointers

**If the bakery dough is difficult** to work with, let it stand at room temperature before shaping it.

**If you'd like a crispy crust,** bake the pizza on the bottom rack of the oven.

**Use a pizza stone** to cook the pizza if you have one. Preheat oven to 450° (keep pizza stone in oven as it preheats). Heat at least 15 minutes before baking the pizza.

**Use a pizza wheel** or kitchen shears to slice the pizza.

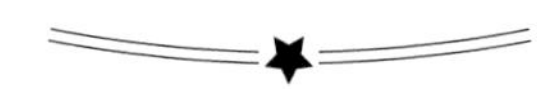

Greek Pizza

# Holiday Dessert Party

*Treat friends and family to something special this season with a gathering devoted completely to showstopping sweets. From red velvet to individual cupcakes—there's something to satisfy every sweet tooth.*

THE MENU
Holiday Dessert Party
serves 8 to 10
MOCHA BAKED ALASKA
RASPBERRY DACQUOISE
COCONUT CAKE ROULADE
TRIPLE COCONUT RUM CHEESECAKE
RED VELVET-RASPBERRY
TIRAMISÙ TRIFLE
INDIVIDUAL PINEAPPLE CAKES WITH
CREAM CHEESE FROSTING
RED VELVET MARBLE BUNDT CAKE
PECAN MILK PUNCH

Raspberry Dacquoise

# MOCHA BAKED ALASKA

**MAKES 24 SERVINGS**
**HANDS-ON 22 MIN. TOTAL 14 HOURS, 42 MIN.**

MOCHA CAKE

Parchment paper
1 cup all-purpose flour
1 cup sugar
⅓ cup Dutch process cocoa
1 tsp. baking soda
½ tsp. baking powder
½ tsp. table salt
½ cup buttermilk
¼ cup vegetable oil
1 large egg
1 tsp. vanilla extract
½ cup brewed coffee
4 cups coffee ice cream, softened
6 cups chocolate ice cream, softened

MARSHMALLOW MERINGUE

6 large egg whites
1 tsp. vanilla extract
¼ tsp. table salt
½ cup sugar
2 (7-oz.) jars marshmallow crème

1. Prepare Mocha Cake: Preheat oven to 350°. Lightly grease a 9-inch round cake pan. Line bottom with parchment paper; lightly grease and flour pan.
2. Sift together flour and next 5 ingredients into a large bowl. Whisk together buttermilk and next 3 ingredients in a small bowl. Add buttermilk mixture to flour mixture; whisk until blended. Gradually add coffee, whisking until blended. Pour batter into prepared pan (batter will be thin). Bake at 350° for 25 minutes or until a wooden pick inserted in center comes out clean. Cool in pan on a wire rack 10 minutes; remove from pan to wire rack, and cool completely (about 1 hour).
3. While cake bakes, line a 2½-qt. bowl (about 9 inches in diameter) with 2 layers of plastic wrap, allowing 2 to 3 inches to extend over sides. Freeze 15 minutes. Spoon coffee ice cream into bottom of chilled bowl and smooth top; freeze 2 hours. Spoon chocolate ice cream over coffee ice cream, and smooth top. Freeze 1 hour.
4. Place cooled cake over chocolate ice cream, pressing gently and trimming to fit as needed. Wrap cake in plastic overhang; freeze 8 hours or overnight.
5. Just before serving, prepare Marshmallow Meringue: Preheat oven to 450°. Beat egg whites and next 2 ingredients at high speed with a heavy-duty electric stand mixer until foamy. Gradually add sugar, 1 Tbsp. at a time, beating until stiff peaks form and sugar dissolves (about 2 to 4 minutes).
6. Beat one-fourth of marshmallow crème into egg white mixture; repeat 3 times with remaining marshmallow crème, beating until smooth (about 1 minute).
7. Invert ice cream cake onto an ovenproof serving plate; remove plastic wrap. Quickly spread Marshmallow Meringue over entire surface, sealing completely. Bake at 450° for 4 to 5 minutes or until golden. Serve immediately.

# RASPBERRY DACQUOISE

**MAKES 10 SERVINGS**
**HANDS-ON 20 MIN. TOTAL 12 HOURS, 20 MIN.**

Parchment paper
1⅔ cups whole blanched almonds
1½ cups plus 4½ Tbsp. granulated sugar, divided
3 Tbsp. cornstarch
12 large egg whites
¾ tsp. cream of tartar
1½ tsp. vanilla extract
1 tsp. almond extract
3½ cups whipping cream
½ cup powdered sugar
¼ cup black raspberry liqueur
5 cups fresh raspberries, divided
Garnish: fresh mint, pomegranate seeds

1. Preheat oven to 200°. Line 3 large baking sheets with parchment paper. Draw 2 (8-inch) circles on each piece of parchment; turn parchment over.
2. Pulse almonds, 4½ Tbsp. sugar, and cornstarch in a food processor until finely ground.
3. Beat egg whites at high speed with a heavy-duty electric stand mixer until foamy; add cream of tartar, vanilla, and almond extract, beating until blended. Gradually add remaining 1½ cups granulated sugar, 1 Tbsp. at a time, beating until stiff peaks form and sugar dissolves (about 2 to 4 minutes). Gently fold in almond mixture in 3 additions. Pipe mixture in concentric circles using a ½-inch-round tip onto parchment paper circles.
4. Bake at 200° for 4 hours or until meringues are dry. Turn off oven; let meringues remain in closed oven overnight. Carefully remove meringues from parchment paper.
5. Beat whipping cream, powdered sugar, and liqueur at high speed with an electric mixer until stiff peaks form. Reserve 1½ cups sweetened whipped cream for top of cake.
6. To assemble cake, place 1 meringue layer on a serving plate. Spread one-fifth of whipped cream mixture over meringue. Top with berries. Repeat layers 4 times. Serve immediately.

Coconut Cake Roulade

# COCONUT CAKE ROULADE

**MAKES 8 SERVINGS HANDS-ON 43 MIN.**
**TOTAL 1 HOUR, 35 MIN., PLUS 1 DAY FOR CHILLING**

Parchment paper
1 cup all-purpose flour
1 tsp. baking powder
¼ tsp. table salt
4 large eggs, separated
1¼ cups granulated sugar, divided
1 tsp. vanilla extract
½ tsp. coconut extract
3 Tbsp. powdered sugar
1 coconut, grated
½ cup sour cream
1 (8-oz.) container frozen whipped topping, thawed

**1.** Preheat oven to 375°. Grease bottom and sides of a 15- x 10-inch jelly-roll pan; line with parchment paper. Grease and flour parchment paper. Set aside.
**2.** Combine flour, baking powder, and salt, stirring well. Set aside.
**3.** Beat egg whites at high speed with an electric mixer until foamy. Gradually add ¼ cup granulated sugar, 1 Tbsp. at a time, beating until stiff peaks form and sugar dissolves (about 2 to 4 minutes). Set aside.
**4.** Beat egg yolks in a large bowl at high speed with an electric mixer; gradually add ½ cup granulated sugar. Beat 5 minutes or until thick and pale. Add ⅓ cup water and extracts; beat well. Add flour mixture, and beat just until blended. Fold in one-third egg white mixture. Gently fold in remaining egg white mixture. Spread batter evenly into prepared pan.
**5.** Bake at 375° for 10 to 12 minutes or until top springs back when lightly touched.
**6.** Sift 3 Tbsp. powdered sugar in a 15- x 10-inch rectangle on a cloth towel; set aside.
**7.** Loosen edges of cake from pan. Invert warm cake onto prepared towel. Carefully remove parchment paper, and discard. Starting at 1 short side, roll up cake and towel together; cool completely on a wire rack, seam side down.
**8.** Combine 1 cup grated coconut, remaining ½ cup granulated sugar, and sour cream in a large bowl. Divide sour cream mixture in half. Combine one-half of sour cream mixture with ½ cup whipped topping.
**9.** Unroll cake, and remove towel. Spread whipped topping mixture over top of prepared cake, leaving a 1-inch border, and roll up, jelly-roll fashion, ending seam side down.
**10.** Combine remaining sour cream mixture, 1 cup grated coconut, and remaining whipped topping. Spread mixture evenly over cake roll. Sprinkle with additional grated fresh coconut. Cover and refrigerate 24 hours.

**NOTE:** Fresh coconut adds a special touch to this festive cake. Pierce 2 coconut eyes with an ice pick and hammer; drain liquid, and reserve for another use. Place coconut in a 9-inch cake pan. Bake at 350° for 25 minutes or until shell begins to crack; cool 10 minutes. Break open the outer shell with a hammer, and split coconut into several large pieces. Separate coconut meat from the shell using a sturdy, blunt-ended knife, and rinse in cold water. Cut thin strips from the meat using a vegetable peeler. Use immediately, or layer between damp paper towels in an airtight container, and chill up to 2 days.

# TRIPLE COCONUT RUM CHEESECAKE

**MAKES 12 SERVINGS**
**HANDS-ON 12 MIN. TOTAL 6 HOURS, 37 MIN.**

1 (6.4-oz.) package coconut cookies, finely crushed
¼ cup melted butter
1 cup sugar, divided
5 (8-oz.) packages cream cheese, softened
1 (16-oz.) can cream of coconut
1 tsp. vanilla extract
¼ cup coconut rum, divided
3 large eggs
2 cups toasted sweetened flaked coconut, divided
1½ cups whipping cream

**1.** Preheat oven to 350°. Stir together crushed cookies, melted butter, and ¼ cup sugar; press mixture on bottom and up sides of a 10-inch springform pan coated with cooking spray.
**2.** Bake at 350° for 10 minutes. Cool on a wire rack. Reduce oven temperature to 325°.
**3.** Beat cream cheese and remaining ¾ cup sugar at medium speed with a heavy-duty electric stand mixer until blended. Add cream of coconut, vanilla, and 2 Tbsp. rum, beating at low speed until blended. Add eggs, 1 at a time, beating just until yellow disappears after each addition. Fold in 1 cup toasted coconut.
**4.** Pour batter into prepared crust.
**5.** Bake at 325° for 1 hour and 15 minutes or until center is almost set. Remove cheesecake from oven; gently run a knife around edge of cheesecake to loosen. Cool on a wire rack 1 hour. Cover and chill 4 hours. Remove sides of pan.
**6.** Beat whipping cream and remaining 2 Tbsp. rum at high speed with an electric mixer until soft peaks form. Spread evenly over cheesecake; sprinkle with remaining 1 cup toasted coconut.

**NOTE:** We tested with Pepperidge Farm Coconut Cookies.

Red Velvet-Raspberry Tiramisù Trifle

# RED VELVET-RASPBERRY TIRAMISÙ TRIFLE

**MAKES 12 SERVINGS**
**HANDS-ON 20 MIN. TOTAL 4 HOURS, 20 MIN.**

1 cup seedless raspberry jam
¼ cup black raspberry liqueur
¼ cup fresh orange juice
2 (8-oz.) containers mascarpone cheese
2 cups heavy cream
⅓ cup sugar
1 tsp. vanilla extract
Red Velvet Cake, cut into ¾-inch pieces
3 (6-oz.) containers fresh raspberries
Garnish: fresh mint

1. Whisk together first 3 ingredients in a small bowl.
2. Place mascarpone cheese in a large bowl. Beat heavy cream at high speed with an electric mixer until foamy; gradually add sugar and vanilla, beating until soft peaks form. Stir one-fourth of whipped cream into mascarpone using a rubber spatula; fold in remaining whipped cream.
3. Arrange about ⅓ cup cake pieces in 12 individual trifle dishes; drizzle with about 1 Tbsp. jam mixture, top with raspberries, and dollop with about ¼ cup mascarpone mixture. Repeat layers. Cover and chill 4 to 24 hours before serving.

## RED VELVET CAKE

**MAKES 12 SERVINGS**
**HANDS-ON 15 MIN. TOTAL 1 HOUR, 20 MIN.**

¾ cup granulated sugar
3 large eggs
2 large egg yolks
1 tsp. vanilla extract
¾ cup butter, melted
2 Tbsp. red liquid food coloring
1⅓ cups cake flour
2 Tbsp. unsweetened cocoa
½ tsp. baking powder
¼ tsp. table salt

1. Preheat oven to 350°. Beat first 4 ingredients at medium-high speed with an electric mixer 5 minutes or until thick and pale. Add butter and food coloring, beating until blended.
2. Sift together cake flour and next 3 ingredients; fold into egg mixture. Spoon batter into a lightly greased 13-x 9-inch pan. Bake at 350° for 20 to 25 minutes or until a wooden pick inserted in center comes out clean. Cool 10 minutes. Turn out of pan onto a wire rack. Cool completely.

# INDIVIDUAL PINEAPPLE CAKES WITH CREAM CHEESE FROSTING

**MAKES 2 DOZEN**
**HANDS-ON 20 MIN. TOTAL 4 HOURS, 41 MIN.**

*Guests will never believe that this dessert is made from a cake mix since the lick-your-finger frosting is so decadent. (Pictured on page 74)*

FILLING
½ cup granulated sugar
3 Tbsp. cornstarch
1 (20-oz.) can crushed pineapple in juice, undrained
¼ cup pineapple juice
3 Tbsp. butter

CAKE
24 paper baking cups
1 (16.25-oz.) box white cake mix

FROSTING
1 cup butter, softened
1 (8-oz.) package cream cheese, softened
5 cups powdered sugar
2 tsp. vanilla extract
Garnishes: fresh pineapple wedges, fresh cranberries

1. Prepare Filling: Whisk together granulated sugar, cornstarch, crushed pineapple, and pineapple juice in a medium saucepan. Bring to a boil over medium heat, whisking constantly. Boil, whisking constantly, 1 to 1½ minutes or until thickened. Remove from heat; stir in butter. Pour mixture into a bowl. Place heavy-duty plastic wrap directly on warm filling (to prevent a film from forming); chill 3 to 24 hours.
2. Prepare Cake: Preheat oven to 350°. Place paper baking cups in 2 (12-cup) muffin pans, and coat with cooking spray. Prepare cake mix according to package directions for cupcakes. Spoon cake batter into cups, filling two-thirds full.
3. Bake at 350° for 16 minutes or until a wooden pick inserted in center comes out clean. Cool in pans on wire racks 5 minutes; remove from pans, and cool completely (about 1 hour).
4. Prepare Frosting: Beat butter and cream cheese at medium speed with an electric mixer until creamy. Gradually add powdered sugar, beating until light and fluffy. Beat in vanilla.
5. Place 1¼ cups filling in a large decorating bag fitted with a large round tip. Cut cupcakes in half and squeeze frosting on top of bottom halves. Top cupcakes with top halves.
6. Spoon frosting into a large decorating bag fitted with a large star tip. Pipe frosting on top of cupcakes.

# RED VELVET MARBLE BUNDT CAKE

**MAKES 10 TO 12 SERVINGS**
**HANDS-ON 30 MIN. TOTAL 2 HOURS, 45 MIN.**

- 1 cup butter, softened
- ½ cup shortening
- 2½ cups sugar
- 6 large eggs
- 3 cups all-purpose flour
- 1 tsp. baking powder
- ½ tsp. table salt
- ¾ cup milk
- 1 tsp. vanilla extract
- 1 Tbsp. unsweetened cocoa
- 1 Tbsp. red liquid food coloring
- Snowy White Vanilla Glaze
- Garnish: crushed hard peppermint candies

**1.** Preheat oven to 325°. Beat butter and shortening at medium speed with a heavy-duty electric stand mixer until creamy. Gradually add sugar, beating until light and fluffy. Add eggs, 1 at a time, beating just until blended after each addition.

**2.** Stir together flour and next 2 ingredients. Add to butter mixture alternately with milk, beginning and ending with flour mixture. Beat at low speed just until blended after each addition. Stir in vanilla. Transfer 2 ½ cups batter to a 2-qt. bowl; stir in cocoa and food coloring.

**3.** Drop 2 scoops of plain batter into a greased and floured 10-inch (16-cup) Bundt pan, using a small cookie scoop (about 1 ½ inches); top with 1 scoop of red velvet batter. Repeat around entire pan, covering bottom completely. Continue layering batters in pan as directed until all batter is used.

**4.** Bake at 325° for 1 hour to 1 hour and 5 minutes or until a long wooden pick inserted in center comes out clean. Cool in pan on a wire rack 10 minutes; remove from pan to wire rack, and cool completely (about 1 hour). Drizzle with glaze.

## SNOWY WHITE VANILLA GLAZE

**MAKES ABOUT 1 CUP**
**HANDS-ON 5 MIN. TOTAL 5 MIN.**

**1.** Whisk together 2 ½ cups powdered sugar, 3 Tbsp. plus 1 tsp. milk, and 1 tsp. vanilla extract until smooth.

# PECAN MILK PUNCH

**MAKES 2 CUPS**
**HANDS-ON 15 MIN. TOTAL 3 HOURS, 15 MIN.**

1 cup chopped toasted pecans
½ cup cane syrup
1 Tbsp. cream of coconut
1 tsp. ground cinnamon
½ tsp. vanilla extract
⅛ tsp. kosher salt
¼ cup bourbon
Garnishes: sweetened whipped cream, cinnamon sticks

**1.** Process pecans, syrup, cream of coconut, cinnamon, vanilla, and kosher salt in a food processor 30 to 60 seconds or until smooth. With processor running, pour 1 cup water through food chute. Press mixture through a fine wire-mesh strainer into a pitcher, using back of spoon. Discard solids. Cover and chill 3 to 24 hours. Stir in bourbon just before serving. Serve over ice.

# SWEET SHIMMER

Reflective materials, repeated throughout, add elegance and luster to this holiday dessert party setup.

## 1 SHINE ON

Fruit garnishes fill a trio of small bowls embellished with silver circles and dots, adding color to the table.

## 2 BOXES AND BOWS

Empty boxes wrapped in glittery paper and tied with glimmering gold ribbon create a focal point behind the buffet table.

## 3 GREEN AND GOLD

Rimmed or dipped in gold, white porcelain plates and bowls with organic shapes feel modern. Emerald green accents keep things fresh and festive.

4

LIGHT AND BRIGHT

Snowy white blooms accented with evergreen clippings fill a shallow dish striped in gold.

# Decorate

# Wreath Wonder

*A lasting symbol of the holiday season, the wreath has roots dating back to the Roman Empire where it signified victory. It is as enduring a holiday tradition as it can be varied in design. While a ring of hardy evergreen or laurel boughs is its classic form, let the ideas found here inspire new approaches.*

Showcase favorite family heirlooms, such as these silver trays, by embellishing them with holiday greenery and ribbon.

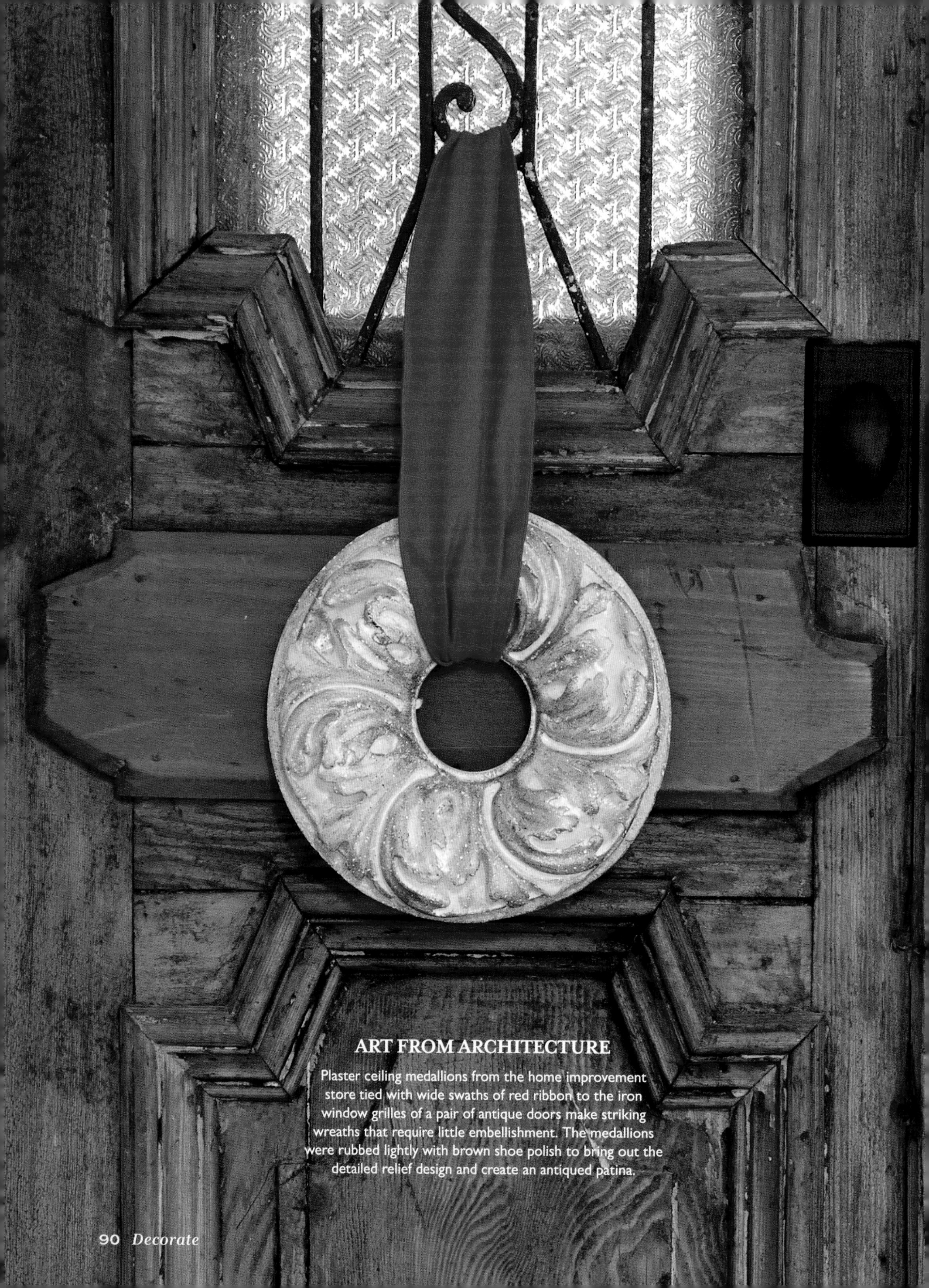

## ART FROM ARCHITECTURE

Plaster ceiling medallions from the home improvement store tied with wide swaths of red ribbon to the iron window grilles of a pair of antique doors make striking wreaths that require little embellishment. The medallions were rubbed lightly with brown shoe polish to bring out the detailed relief design and create an antiqued patina.

## WOODSY WELCOME

Lush and lovely, a pinecone wreath settles into a nest of evergreen clippings, burlap ribbon, and brass bells. Thin brown rope is used to tie the smaller pinecone wreath to the larger one.

## FRAME THE ENTRY

A red lacquered frame embellished with greenery, garland, and pinecones becomes a linear wreath that mimics window and door. A staple gun helps to attach the greenery garland to the frame.

LUSH AND LOVELY

Abundant accents of fruit and berries make this natural wreath a showstopper. Wire picks are useful in attaching fruit to the wreath.

# EVERGREEN DREAM

A wreath to withstand the years and the elements, this welcoming symbol of dried moss and preserved lichen dyed green is a vibrant nod to the traditional.

1

## WOODSY WONDER

Preserved botanicals, such as reindeer, Spanish, and sheet moss combined with dried lichen, form a wreath that makes a lasting impression.

2

## INGREDIENTS FOR IMPACT

A flat straw wreath form is camouflaged with sheet moss, then topped with an artful arrangement of preserved botanicals using hot glue and a textured ribbon accent.

# Trees with a Twist

*Whether you trim the tree or make a tree from trimmings, there are many ways to create festive holiday decor. Deck the traditional evergreen tree or reinterpret pieces you already have with a few unexpected flourishes to last the holiday season and garner oohs and aahs.*

## TREE STAND

Nothing marks the beginning of the season like the arrival of the Christmas tree. While many are bought at the tree lot or carried down in a box from the attic, there's also the chance to create a whimsical tree such as this one made from a metal-mesh étagère filled with hypericum berries, boxwood, evergreen, magnolia, and cypress clippings.

# OUTDOORS IN

Boughs, berries, blossoms, and boxes tied with twine combine with fruit in the perfect holiday vignette for small spaces.

1

## BERRY MERRY

Leafless ilex or possumhaw branches are striking on their own or in arrangements.

2

## A-TISKET A-TASKET

This flower-berry-and-cypress-filled basket lasts weeks thanks to wet florist foam and a plastic liner.

3

## ARTFUL GIFTS

Christmas presents can also be used as holiday decorations.

4

## DRESS THE WALLS

No sense letting vertical spaces go to waste. A wall tree is a striking addition to any space—small apartment or grand estate.

# Mantel Magic

*The hearth is the gathering place for fireside stories and reminiscences as well as winter naps and goodies for Santa. Make this holiday beacon beautiful, whether you go natural, minimal, or whimsical.*

## SOUTHERN CHARM

A garland of magnolia, greenery, apples, and kumquats brings vibrant Christmas color to the mantel. Fireballs, which are similar to gas logs, add ambience to the look.

## MERRY AND BRIGHT

Give favorite holiday trinkets a new look by combining them with miniature brightly wrapped packages and grouping them together in unique ways.

## WINTER WHITE

A muted palette of beige, gray, and metallics can lend a warm-yet-sophisticated feel to a mantel. Use flowers and greenery to soften the effect.

# Savor

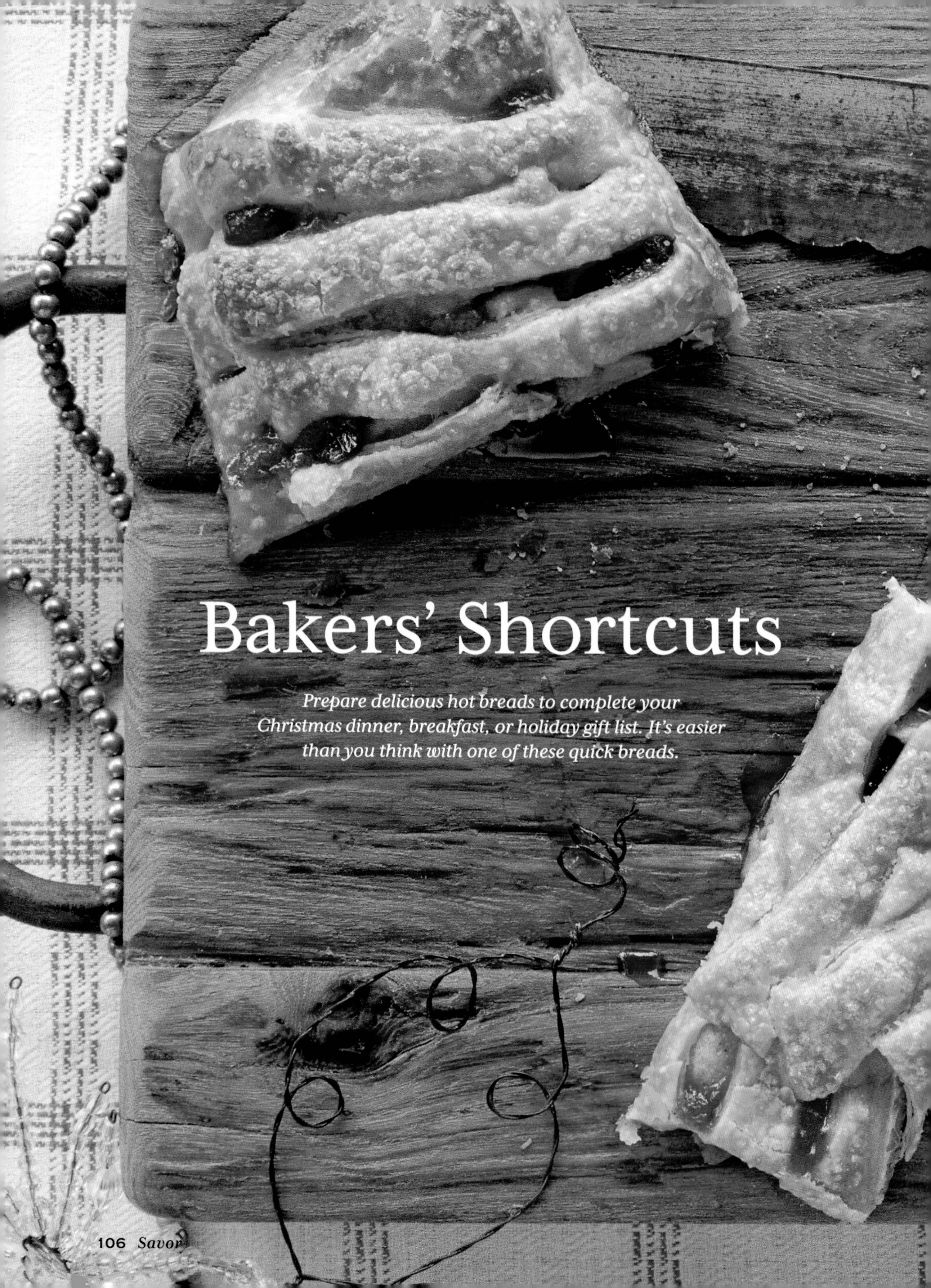

# Bakers' Shortcuts

*Prepare delicious hot breads to complete your Christmas dinner, breakfast, or holiday gift list. It's easier than you think with one of these quick breads.*

CLAUSS

Bacon-Apple-Cheddar Doughnuts
Easy Cinnamon Rolls
Orange-Spiral Sweet Rolls

# ORANGE-SPIRAL SWEET ROLLS

**MAKES 2 DOZEN**
**HANDS-ON 20 MIN. TOTAL 1 HOUR, 41 MIN.**

*Start a new holiday breakfast tradition with these fragrant orange sweet rolls.*

1 (32-oz.) package frozen bread roll dough, thawed
1¼ cups orange marmalade
½ cup butter, softened
⅔ cup firmly packed brown sugar
1 orange
1½ cups powdered sugar
1 Tbsp. whipping cream
Garnish: orange zest

**1.** Roll dough into a 15- x 10-inch rectangle on a lightly floured surface. Stir together orange marmalade and butter; spread onto dough rectangle, leaving a 1-inch border. Sprinkle brown sugar evenly over butter mixture. Roll up, jelly-roll fashion, starting at 1 long side. Pinch edges of seam to seal.
**2.** Cut roll into 1-inch-thick slices, and place slices in 2 lightly greased 9-inch cake pans with sides touching. Cover and let rise in a warm place (80° to 85°), free from drafts, 1 to 1½ hours or until doubled in bulk.
**3.** Preheat oven to 375°. Bake at 375° for 16 to 17 minutes or until golden brown. Cool in pans on wire racks 5 minutes. Invert rolls onto 2 serving platters.
**4.** Meanwhile, grate zest from orange to equal 2 tsp. Cut orange in half; squeeze juice from orange into a measuring cup to equal 3 Tbsp. Stir together orange juice, 1 tsp. orange zest, powdered sugar, and whipping cream until smooth; drizzle over tops of rolls.

# EASY CINNAMON ROLLS

**MAKES 8 SERVINGS**
**HANDS-ON 10 MIN. TOTAL 33 MIN.**

*If you can't find the crescent roll dough sheet, purchase crescent roll dough and pinch all of the perforations to seal.*

⅓ cup granulated sugar
1½ tsp. ground cinnamon
2 (8-oz.) cans refrigerated crescent roll dough sheet
¼ cup butter, melted
¾ cup powdered sugar
2 to 3 Tbsp. whipping cream
½ tsp. vanilla extract

**1.** Preheat oven to 375°. Combine granulated sugar and cinnamon in a small bowl.
**2.** Unroll 1 dough sheet onto work surface; top with second dough sheet, and press firmly. Brush with butter; sprinkle with cinnamon-sugar mixture. Roll up tightly, jelly-roll fashion, starting at 1 long side. Cut into 8 slices. Place slices into 8 greased muffin cups. Brush tops with remaining melted butter.
**3.** Bake at 375° for 18 to 20 minutes or until golden brown.
**4.** Meanwhile, whisk together powdered sugar, whipping cream, and vanilla in a small bowl until smooth.
**5.** Remove rolls from muffin cups; cool 5 minutes. Top with glaze; serve warm.

# BACON-APPLE-CHEDDAR DOUGHNUTS

**MAKES 20 SERVINGS**
**HANDS-ON 25 MIN. TOTAL 25 MIN.**

*Applewood-smoked bacon and cheese add a smoky flavor to these doughnuts and complement the sweetness of the apple. Smoked Gouda would also pair well instead of Cheddar.*

6 applewood-smoked bacon slices
½ cup chopped Fuji apple
2 Tbsp. chopped sweet onion
Vegetable oil
1 (12-oz.) can refrigerated buttermilk biscuits
½ cup (2 oz.) freshly shredded applewood-smoked Cheddar cheese
1 cup powdered sugar
2 Tbsp. apple juice

**1.** Cook bacon in a large skillet over medium-high heat 5 to 6 minutes or until crisp; remove bacon, and drain on paper towels, reserving 1 Tbsp. drippings in skillet. Crumble bacon.
**2.** Sauté apple and onion in hot drippings 2 minutes or until tender. Place apple mixture in a small bowl. Stir in half of crumbled bacon. Set aside.
**3.** Pour oil to depth of 2 inches into a Dutch oven; heat to 375°.
**4.** Separate dough into 10 biscuits; cut each biscuit in half crosswise. Press each half into a 2-inch circle. Place about 1 tsp. reserved bacon mixture in center of dough. Top with about 1 tsp. cheese. Fold dough over cheese; gently press edges of dough to seal completely.
**5.** Fry biscuits in hot oil, in batches, 2 minutes or until golden brown. Drain on paper towels.
**6.** Whisk together powdered sugar and juice in small bowl. Drizzle over doughnuts. Sprinkle with remaining bacon.

# CINNAMON-PECAN FAN BREAD

**MAKES 8 TO 10 SERVINGS**
**HANDS-ON 25 MIN. TOTAL 2 HOURS, 20 MIN.**

*For an over-the-top treat, drizzle with your favorite cinnamon roll icing.*

⅔ cup granulated sugar
⅔ cup firmly packed brown sugar
3½ tsp. ground cinnamon
1 (25-oz.) package frozen Parkerhouse-style roll dough, thawed
¾ cup butter, melted
¾ cup chopped pecans

**1.** Combine first 3 ingredients in a small bowl. Press or roll each piece of dough into a 3-inch square. Brush each piece generously with melted butter; sprinkle with pecans, pressing into dough. Sprinkle generously with cinnamon-sugar mixture. Stack one-fourth of squares; set aside. Repeat with remaining dough, pecans, and cinnamon-sugar mixture to make 3 additional stacks. Place stacks of dough vertically into a well-greased 9- x 5-inch loaf pan to resemble a fan.
**2.** Cover and let rise in a warm place (80° to 85°), free from drafts, 1 hour or until doubled in bulk.
**3.** Preheat oven to 375°. Place loaf pan on an aluminum foil-lined baking pan.
**4.** Bake at 375° for 30 to 35 minutes or until golden brown, shielding with aluminum foil after 20 minutes to prevent excessive browning. Cool in pan on a wire rack 10 minutes; remove from pan to wire rack, and cool 15 minutes. Serve warm or at room temperature.

# PEAR-WALNUT PULL-APART LOAF

**MAKES 8 SERVINGS**
**HANDS-ON 12 MIN. TOTAL 1 HOUR, 12 MIN.**

*This pear-packed pull-apart loaf is filled with sticky sweet goodness and made easy with refrigerated buttermilk biscuits.*

- 1 (16.3-oz.) can refrigerated jumbo buttermilk biscuits
- ½ cup butter, melted
- ½ tsp. vanilla extract
- 1 cup firmly packed brown sugar
- ¾ cup finely chopped walnuts
- 2 tsp. ground cinnamon
- 1 cup chopped peeled Anjou pear

**1.** Preheat oven to 350°. Cut biscuits into quarters.
**2.** Combine melted butter and vanilla in a small bowl. Combine brown sugar, walnuts, and cinnamon in a shallow bowl. Coat half of biscuit pieces in butter mixture; dredge pieces in brown sugar mixture. Arrange in a lightly greased 9- x 5-inch loaf pan; top with chopped pears. Repeat procedure with remaining biscuit pieces, butter mixture, and brown sugar mixture. Arrange biscuit pieces over pears.
**3.** Bake at 350° for 40 to 45 minutes or until golden brown. Cool in pan on a wire rack 10 minutes; invert onto a serving plate, and cool 10 minutes. Serve warm.

# CRANBERRY-APPLE STRUDEL

**MAKES 6 SERVINGS**
**HANDS-ON 13 MIN. TOTAL 53 MIN.**

*Breakfast or dessert? Let your family decide. Add a simple powdered sugar glaze for an even sweeter treat. Depending on the quality of the crystallized ginger, you may want to use only 2 tsp. if the ginger is strong.* *(Pictured on page 106)*

- 2 cups thinly sliced peeled Fuji apples
- ⅓ cup sweetened dried cranberries
- ⅓ cup firmly packed brown sugar
- 1 Tbsp. all-purpose flour
- 1 Tbsp. chopped crystallized ginger
- ¼ tsp. ground cinnamon
- ½ (17.3-oz.) package frozen puff pastry sheets, thawed
- Parchment paper
- 1 large egg, lightly beaten
- 1 Tbsp. turbinado sugar

**1.** Preheat oven to 400°. Combine first 6 ingredients in a medium bowl; toss to combine.
**2.** Roll pastry sheet into a 14- x 12-inch rectangle on a lightly floured surface, and place on a parchment paper-lined baking sheet. Spoon apple mixture lengthwise down center of pastry. Cut slits 1 inch apart from 2 long sides of pastry rectangle to within ½ inch of apple mixture. Starting at 1 end, fold pastry strips over apple mixture, alternating sides, to cover apple mixture. Brush top of pastry with beaten egg; sprinkle with turbinado sugar.
**3.** Bake at 400° for 25 to 30 minutes or until pastry is deep golden brown and apples are tender. Cool on pan on a wire rack 15 minutes. Serve warm, or cool completely (about 1 hour).

# DUKKAH MEZZE DINNER ROLLS

**MAKES 2 DOZEN**
**HANDS-ON 10 MIN. TOTAL 35 MIN.**

*Mezze is a selection of small plates and drinks served at the beginning of Middle Eastern meals. In Egypt, it typically includes dukkah—a mix of nuts, seeds, and spices used for flavoring pita bread and vegetables that have been dipped in olive oil. These buttery rolls will delight dinner guests with their nutty, exotic flavors.*

¼ cup sesame seeds
2 Tbsp. garbanzo bean flour
2 Tbsp. blanched hazelnuts
2 Tbsp. coriander seeds
1 Tbsp. cumin seeds
½ tsp. dried thyme
½ tsp. kosher salt
¼ tsp. black peppercorns
2 (8-oz.) cans refrigerated crescent roll dough sheet
½ cup butter, melted
Parchment paper

**1.** Preheat oven to 375°. Heat sesame seeds, garbanzo bean flour, and next 3 ingredients in a small nonstick skillet over medium-low heat, stirring often, 3 minutes or until toasted and fragrant. Cool 10 minutes; place in a spice grinder or food processor. Add thyme, salt, and peppercorns; process 2 to 3 seconds to create a coarse mixture. Set aside ¼ cup spice mixture.
**2.** Unroll crescent dough sheets. Brush half of melted butter over both sheets of dough; sprinkle with spice mixture, and roll up, jelly-roll fashion, starting at 1 long side, ending seam sides down.
**3.** Cut each roll into 12 slices; place on parchment paper-lined baking sheets.
**4.** Bake at 375° for 15 minutes or until golden brown; brush with remaining butter, and sprinkle with reserved ¼ cup spice mixture. Serve warm.

# SPICY CHEESE STRAWS

**MAKES ABOUT 17 DOZEN**
**HANDS-ON 35 MIN. TOTAL 1 HOUR, 31 MIN.**

*These easy cheese straws make an extra-large batch, so you'll have enough for snacks, gifts, and everything in between. Store in an airtight container in the refrigerator.*

1 (11-oz.) package piecrust mix
¾ cup buttermilk
2 cups shredded sharp Cheddar cheese
1 cup shredded white Cheddar cheese
1 tsp. ground red pepper
⅛ tsp. smoked paprika
Parchment paper
½ cup grated Parmesan cheese

**1.** Preheat oven to 350°. Beat piecrust mix and buttermilk at medium speed with a heavy-duty electric stand mixer until blended. Add cheeses, red pepper, and paprika. Beat just until combined; form dough into a ball.
**2.** Use a cookie press with a star-shaped disk to shape mixture into 2- to 3-inch ribbons, following manufacturer's instructions, on parchment paper-lined baking sheets. Sprinkle evenly with Parmesan cheese.
**3.** Bake at 350° for 14 minutes or until lightly browned. Remove to wire racks to cool.

**NOTE:** We tested with Betty Crocker Piecrust Mix.

**HOLIDAY HINTS**

## Cheese-Straw Tricks

**Shred your own cheese;** it's stickier and blends better than preshredded cheese.

**Refrigerate unbaked dough** between batches to keep straws from spreading too thin when baked.

**Store baked cheese straws** in an airtight container in the refrigerator for 1 week. Store unbaked dough in the fridge for 1 week or in the freezer for 1 month.

**Bake stored cheese straws** in the oven at 350° for 3 to 4 minutes to make them crispy again.

Spicy Cheese Straws

Cheesy Onion and Bacon
Monkey Bread

# CHEESY ONION AND BACON MONKEY BREAD

**MAKES 16 SERVINGS**
**HANDS-ON 44 MIN. TOTAL 2 HOURS, 29 MIN.**

*This savory monkey bread packed full of caramelized onions, Gruyère cheese, and bacon makes a great breakfast treat, as well as an accompaniment with soups and salads.*

5 Tbsp. butter, divided
2 sweet onions, halved and vertically sliced
1 (32-oz.) package frozen bread dough, thawed according to package instructions
1⅓ cups cooked and crumbled bacon slices (about 14)
2 cups shredded Gruyère cheese

**1.** Melt 2 Tbsp. butter in a large skillet over medium heat. Add sliced onions. Cook, stirring often, 15 to 20 minutes or until onions are caramel colored.
**2.** Divide dough into thirds. Shape each dough portion into 16 balls.
**3.** Microwave remaining 3 Tbsp. butter in a small microwave-safe bowl at HIGH 30 seconds or until melted. Sprinkle ⅓ cup bacon in bottom of a lightly greased 12-cup Bundt pan. Sprinkle with ½ cup cheese. Arrange one-third of the dough balls over cheese; brush with melted butter. Arrange half of the caramelized onions over dough. Sprinkle with ⅓ cup bacon and ½ cup cheese. Repeat layers once. Top with remaining dough balls; brush with remaining melted butter. Sprinkle with remaining ⅓ cup bacon and ½ cup cheese.
**4.** Cover and let rise in a warm place (80° to 85°), free from drafts, 1 hour to 1½ hours or until doubled in bulk.
**5.** Preheat oven to 350°. Bake at 350° for 35 minutes or until top is golden brown. Cool in pan on a wire rack 10 minutes; carefully invert bread onto a serving platter. Serve warm.

# ROSEMARY OLIVE AND GARLIC LOAF

**MAKES 2 LOAVES**
**HANDS-ON 10 MIN. TOTAL 2 HOURS, 25 MIN.**

*This recipe makes two loaves, one for eating and one for giving in the spirit of the holiday season.*

½ cup olive tapenade, divided
2 garlic cloves, chopped
2 Tbsp. chopped fresh rosemary
1 (32-oz.) package frozen bread dough, thawed according to package instructions
½ cup thinly sliced red onion, divided
1 cup freshly grated Parmigiano-Reggiano cheese, divided
Parchment paper
2 Tbsp. melted butter

**1.** Combine tapenade, garlic, and rosemary in a medium bowl. Roll each dough portion into a 12- x 8-inch rectangle on a lightly floured surface. Spread ¼ cup tapenade mixture on each rectangle, leaving a 1-inch border. Sprinkle ¼ cup red onion and ½ cup cheese on each rectangle.
**2.** Roll up each dough rectangle, starting at 1 short side. Place 1 dough roll, seam side down, on a parchment paper-lined baking sheet. Repeat procedure with second dough rectangle.
**3.** Cover and let rise in a warm place (80° to 85°), free from drafts, 1 hour or until doubled in bulk.
**4.** Preheat oven to 350°. Brush each loaf with 1 Tbsp. melted butter. Bake at 350° for 1 hour or until golden brown, shielding with aluminum foil after 30 minutes to prevent excessive browning. Cool on pan on a wire rack 15 minutes. Serve warm or cool completely.

# Slow-Cooker Sides & Starters

*Make your slow cooker your best friend this time of year. Use this handy appliance to prepare appetizers, beverages, and side dishes for a hands-off approach to cooking that has the added bonus of keeping your oven free for the main dish.*

# SPICED HOT CHOCOLATE

**MAKES 20 SERVINGS**
**HANDS-ON 4 MIN. TOTAL 3 HOURS, 4 MIN.**

*Mezcal is a distilled beverage made from the agave plant and has a distinct smoky flavor. A high-quality tequila can be substituted if Mezcal isn't available at your local liquor store.* *(Pictured on page 116)*

3 cups half-and-half
2 cups milk
1¼ cups Mezcal or tequila
12 oz. dark chocolate, chopped
½ cup agave syrup
¾ tsp. ground cinnamon
¼ tsp. ground chipotle chile pepper or ground red pepper
Garnishes: whipped cream, ground cinnamon

**1.** Combine first 7 ingredients in a 4-qt. slow cooker. Cover and cook on LOW 3 hours, stirring after 2 hours. Whisk well before serving.

# SPICED RUM MULLED CIDER

**MAKES 8 TO 10 SERVINGS**
**HANDS-ON 5 MIN. TOTAL 3 HOURS, 5 MIN.**

*Serve this warm and toasty mulled cider in a tall glass mug to friends and family during the Christmas season.* *(Pictured on page 117)*

4 (3-inch) cinnamon sticks
1 (2-inch) piece peeled fresh ginger, sliced
1 tsp. whole cloves
½ tsp. whole black peppercorns
1 (64-oz.) bottle apple cider
1 navel orange, sliced
1½ cups spiced rum
Garnishes: cinnamon sticks, sliced oranges

**1.** Combine first 6 ingredients in a 3-qt. slow cooker. Cover and cook on LOW 3 hours. Pour liquid through a fine wire-mesh strainer, discarding solids. Stir in rum.

# MEATBALLS IN TOMATO CHUTNEY

**MAKES 18 SERVINGS**
**HANDS-ON 17 MIN. TOTAL 4 HOURS, 32 MIN.**

*Make meatballs the day before, or use frozen, thawed prepared meatballs instead of making your own.*

3 (14½-oz.) cans fire-roasted diced tomatoes with garlic, drained
2 cups chopped onion, divided
1 jalapeño, seeded and chopped
½ cup golden raisins
1 (6-oz.) can tomato sauce
3 Tbsp. tomato paste
½ cup apple cider vinegar
½ cup firmly packed brown sugar
1 tsp. curry powder
1½ tsp. table salt, divided
1 lb. ground Italian pork sausage
1 lb. ground round
¼ cup finely chopped fresh parsley
1 large egg
Garnish: fresh parsley

**1.** Stir together tomatoes, 1½ cups onion, next 7 ingredients, and ½ tsp. salt in a 6-qt. slow cooker coated with cooking spray. Cook, uncovered, on HIGH 3 hours or until thickened.
**2.** Preheat oven to 400°. Meanwhile, combine remaining ½ cup onion, sausage and next 3 ingredients in a large bowl. Shape mixture into 36 (1-inch) balls. Arrange in a single layer on lightly greased rimmed baking sheets. Bake at 400° for 15 minutes or until browned and cooked through.
**3.** Add meatballs to slow cooker. Cover and cook on LOW 1 hour.

**Meatballs in Tomato Chutney**

Asian-Style Riblets

# ASIAN-STYLE RIBLETS

**MAKES 12 SERVINGS**
**HANDS-ON 19 MIN. TOTAL 4 HOURS, 34 MIN.**

*Sweet and spicy Asian-style baby back riblets are best when briefly broiled after slow cooking. If you prefer, ask your butcher to cut slabs of baby back ribs in half lengthwise for riblets. Serve in bowls over fresh slaw, if desired.*

2 slabs baby back pork ribs (about 4 lbs.), cut in half lengthwise
¾ tsp. table salt
1 (10.5-oz.) jar hot pepper jelly
½ cup soy sauce
½ cup rice vinegar
½ cup firmly packed brown sugar
2 Tbsp. dark sesame oil
3 Tbsp. minced fresh ginger
3 large garlic cloves, minced
3 Tbsp. Asian chili-garlic sauce
½ cup chopped green onions
¼ cup chopped fresh cilantro

**1.** Cut riblets into 3-rib portions; sprinkle salt evenly over ribs, and set aside.
**2.** Combine hot pepper jelly and next 8 ingredients in a saucepan. Cook over low heat until jelly melts. Pour half of jelly mixture in a 6-qt. slow cooker. Place ribs in slow cooker; pour remaining jelly mixture over ribs.
**3.** Cover and cook on LOW 4 hours. Remove ribs; skim fat from sauce in slow cooker. Pour sauce into a medium saucepan. Bring to a boil over medium-high heat, and cook until liquid is reduced by half (about 15 minutes). Arrange ribs on a serving platter. Sprinkle with cilantro. Serve with sauce.

# PIMIENTO CHEESE NACHO DIP

**MAKES 40 SERVINGS**
**HANDS-ON 5 MIN. TOTAL 2 HOURS, 35 MIN.**

*As a Southern staple, pimiento cheese is reinvented in this smooth and creamy crowd-pleasing dip.*

1 (3-lb.) block white American cheese, cut into 1-inch cubes
2 (10-oz.) cans diced tomatoes and green chiles, undrained
1 (4-oz.) jar diced pimiento, drained
1¼ cups milk
1 cup chicken broth
1 (12-oz.) container pimiento cheese
2 Tbsp. chopped fresh cilantro
Blue corn tortilla chips

**1.** Stir together first 5 ingredients in a 4-qt. slow cooker.
**2.** Cover and cook on LOW 2½ hours or until melted and smooth. Stir in pimiento cheese; sprinkle with cilantro. Serve with tortilla chips.

**NOTE:** We tested with Palmetto Pimiento Cheese.

**HOLIDAY HINTS**

## Slow-Cooker Secrets

**Make-ahead magic:** If your slow cooker has a removable insert, you can assemble the ingredients for some recipes in the insert the night before, and then refrigerate the whole thing.

**Don't get burned:** Although cooking time is more flexible in a slow cooker than in an oven, over-cooking is possible, so test for doneness close to the time given in the recipe.

**Add, don't stir:** There's no need to stir ingredients unless a recipe specifically calls for it. Just layer the ingredients as the recipe directs.

Orange-Ginger Beets

Slow-Cooked Turnip Greens with Country Ham

Double Pork Green Beans and Potatoes

## SLOW-COOKED TURNIP GREENS WITH COUNTRY HAM

**MAKES 6 SERVINGS**
**HANDS-ON 5 MIN. TOTAL 4 HOURS, 5 MIN.**

*This hands-off approach to cooking turnip greens is perfect for the holidays. Serve with hot pepper sauce, if desired.*

2 (1-lb.) packages chopped fresh turnip greens
8 oz. country ham, chopped
1 (14-oz.) can chicken broth
1 small onion, chopped
2 garlic cloves, crushed
1 Tbsp. apple cider vinegar
1 tsp. sugar

1. Stir together all ingredients in a 7-qt. slow cooker.
2. Cover and cook on LOW 4 hours or until greens are tender, stirring after 2 hours.

## SLOW-COOKER SWEET POTATOES

**MAKES 8 SERVINGS**
**HANDS-ON 20 MIN. TOTAL 3 HOURS, 20 MIN.**

2 (29-oz.) cans sweet potatoes in syrup, drained and mashed (about 4 cups mashed)
⅓ cup butter, melted
½ cup granulated sugar
3 Tbsp. light brown sugar
2 large eggs, lightly beaten
1 tsp. vanilla extract
½ tsp. ground cinnamon
⅓ cup heavy whipping cream
¾ cup chopped pecans
¾ cup firmly packed light brown sugar
¼ cup all-purpose flour
2 Tbsp. butter, melted

1. Combine first 7 ingredients in a large bowl; beat at medium speed with an electric mixer until smooth. Add whipping cream; stir well. Pour into a lightly greased 3-qt. slow cooker.
2. Combine pecans and next 3 ingredients in a small bowl. Sprinkle over sweet potatoes. Cover and cook on HIGH 3 to 4 hours.

**NOTE:** This is a great holiday side that cooks on the stove-top while your turkey and dressing fill your oven.

## DOUBLE PORK GREEN BEANS AND POTATOES

**MAKES 10 SERVINGS**
**HANDS-ON 10 MIN. TOTAL 6 HOURS, 10 MIN.**

*Be sure to serve cornbread on the side to soak up all the flavorful "pot likker" that the green beans cook in. The pork rinds sprinkled on top prior to serving add a bit of crunch and extra pork flavor.*

3 lb. fresh green beans, trimmed
2 cups chopped onion
2 (14-oz.) cans chicken broth
½ tsp. freshly ground black pepper
1 tsp. seasoned salt
2 Tbsp. hot sauce
1 cup chopped country ham (about 5 oz.)
1 lb. baby red potatoes, halved
2 cups pork rinds, lightly crushed

1. Stir together all ingredients, except pork rinds, in a 5-qt. slow cooker.
2. Cover and cook on LOW 6 hours or until green beans and potatoes are very tender.
3. Sprinkle with pork rinds before serving.

## ORANGE-GINGER BEETS

**MAKES 8 TO 10 SERVINGS**
**HANDS-ON 16 MIN. TOTAL 6 HOURS, 16 MIN.**

*Serve these beets over a bed of mixed greens, and top with crumbled goat cheese for a simple salad.*

⅓ cup fresh orange juice
3 Tbsp. honey
2 Tbsp. white wine vinegar
2 Tbsp. olive oil
1 Tbsp. grated fresh ginger
1 tsp. loosely packed orange zest
½ tsp. table salt
¼ tsp. freshly ground black pepper
6 large beets (about 5 lb.), trimmed and peeled

1. Whisk together first 8 ingredients in a small bowl.
2. Place beets in a 5-qt. slow cooker. Pour orange juice mixture over beets. Cover and cook on LOW 6 hours or until beets are tender. Remove beets from slow cooker; when cool enough to handle, slice. Discard any liquid in slow cooker.

# Mains in Minutes

*Start the season off right with stellar entrées. Whether you need something for a casual dinner with family and friends or a special one for Christmas dinner, you're sure to find it here.*

## PORK WITH APPLES, BACON, AND SAUERKRAUT

**MAKES 6 TO 8 SERVINGS**
**HANDS-ON 50 MIN. TOTAL 3 HOURS, 50 MIN.**

*Find pancetta—unsmoked Italian bacon cured with salt and spices—in the deli section. (Pictured on page 125)*

1 (3-lb.) boneless pork loin
½ tsp. kosher salt
½ tsp. freshly ground black pepper
6 oz. thinly sliced pancetta or bacon
Kitchen string
2 Tbsp. olive oil
2 small onions, quartered (root end intact)
1 (12-oz.) package frozen pearl onions (about 2 cups)
2 garlic cloves, thinly sliced
3 fresh thyme sprigs
2 bay leaves
1 (12-oz.) bottle stout or porter beer
2 Tbsp. Dijon mustard
3 firm apples (such as Gala), divided
2 cups jarred sauerkraut, rinsed
2 cups finely shredded green cabbage
1 Tbsp. chopped fresh flat-leaf parsley
1 tsp. fresh lemon juice
½ cup apricot preserves
¼ cup chicken broth

**1.** Trim fat and silver skin from pork. Sprinkle pork with kosher salt and pepper. Wrap top and sides of pork with pancetta. Tie with kitchen string, securing at 1-inch intervals.
**2.** Cook pork in hot oil in a large skillet over medium heat, turning occasionally, 15 minutes or until deep golden brown. Remove from skillet, reserving drippings in skillet.
**3.** Place quartered onion and next 4 ingredients in a 6-qt. slow cooker; top with pork.
**4.** Add beer to reserved drippings in skillet, and cook over medium heat 8 minutes or until liquid is reduced by half, stirring to loosen brown bits from bottom of skillet. Stir in mustard, and pour over pork. Cover and cook on HIGH 2 hours.
**5.** Peel 2 apples, and cut into large wedges. Add apple wedges, sauerkraut, and cabbage to slow cooker; cover and cook 1 to 2 more hours or until a meat thermometer inserted into thickest portion of pork registers 145° and apples are tender.
**6.** Cut remaining unpeeled apple into thin strips, and toss with parsley and lemon juice. Add table salt and freshly ground black pepper to taste.
**7.** Combine preserves and broth in a small saucepan, and cook over medium heat, stirring often, 4 to 5 minutes or until melted and smooth.
**8.** Brush pork with apricot mixture. Cut pork into slices, and serve with onion mixture, apple-parsley mixture, and additional Dijon mustard.

## GINGER-PEACH GLAZED HAM

**MAKES 12 SERVINGS**
**HANDS-ON 7 MIN. TOTAL 1 HOUR, 22 MIN.**

*Jarred peach chutney layers on more flavor and makes easy work of this holiday baked ham.*

1 (9-oz.) jar peach chutney
¼ cup firmly packed brown sugar
¼ cup sorghum syrup
2 tsp. apple cider vinegar
1½ tsp. country-style Dijon mustard
1½ tsp. grated fresh ginger
1 (7- to 8-lb.) fully cooked, bone-in ham

**1.** Preheat oven to 350°. Process first 6 ingredients in a blender or food processor until smooth, stopping to scrape down sides as needed. Reserve ¾ cup chutney mixture to serve with ham.
**2.** Remove skin from ham, and trim fat to ¼-inch thickness. Place ham in an aluminum foil-lined 13- x 9-inch pan. Brush ham with one-third remaining chutney mixture.
**3.** Bake at 350° on lower oven rack 1 hour or until a meat thermometer registers 140°, basting with remaining two-thirds chutney mixture every 20 minutes. Remove from oven, and let stand 15 minutes before serving. Serve with reserved ¾ cup chutney mixture.

**NOTE:** We tested with Neera's Peach Chutney. It can be ordered online.

Ginger-Peach Glazed Ham

Jambalaya

# JAMBALAYA

**MAKES 8 TO 10 SERVINGS**
**HANDS-ON 30 MIN. TOTAL 1 HOUR**

*Build deep flavors by sautéing the aromatic trinity of onion, celery, and pepper in the andouille drippings with herbs, garlic, and spices.*

1 lb. andouille sausage, sliced
2 Tbsp. canola oil
2 cups diced sweet onion
1 cup diced celery
1 large red bell pepper, diced
4 garlic cloves, minced
1 bay leaf
2 tsp. Creole seasoning
1 tsp. dried thyme
1 tsp. dried oregano
2 (10-oz.) cans diced tomatoes and green chiles, drained
3 cups chicken broth
2 cups uncooked long-grain rice
2 cups shredded cooked chicken
1 lb. peeled, medium-size raw shrimp, deveined
½ cup chopped fresh flat-leaf parsley
Garnish: chopped green onions

**1.** Cook sausage in hot oil in a Dutch oven over medium-high heat, stirring constantly, 5 minutes or until browned. Remove sausage with a slotted spoon.
**2.** Add diced onion and next 7 ingredients to hot drippings; sauté 5 minutes or until vegetables are tender. Stir in tomatoes, next 3 ingredients, and sausage. Bring to a boil over high heat. Cover, reduce heat to medium, and simmer, stirring occasionally, 20 minutes or until rice is tender.
**3.** Stir in shrimp; cover and cook 5 minutes or just until shrimp turn pink. Stir in parsley. Serve immediately.

**To Freeze:** Prepare recipe as directed. Line a 13- x 9-inch baking dish with heavy-duty aluminum foil, allowing 2 to 3 inches to extend over sides; spoon jambalaya into prepared dish. Cover and freeze. To serve, remove foil, and place frozen casserole in a lightly greased 13- x 9-inch baking dish; cover and thaw in refrigerator 24 hours. Let stand at room temperature 30 minutes. Bake at 350° until thoroughly heated.

# CHICKEN AND SAUSAGE CASSOULET

**MAKES 4 TO 6 SERVINGS**
**HANDS-ON 14 MIN. TOTAL 34 MIN.**

*Traditional French cassoulet is slow-cooked. Canned vegetables, croutons, and deli-roasted chicken make this version quick and easy and ready in less than an hour.*

1 (14-oz.) package smoked sausage, sliced
1 cup chopped onion
2 garlic cloves, minced
2 cups shredded deli-roasted chicken
1 (15.5-oz.) can cannellini beans, drained and rinsed
1 (14½-oz.) can fire-roasted diced tomatoes, undrained
1 cup chicken broth
½ tsp. table salt
¼ tsp. freshly ground black pepper
2 cups seasoned croutons, crushed
2 Tbsp. butter, melted

**1.** Preheat oven to 350°. Cook sausage and onion in a large Dutch oven over medium-high heat 5 minutes or until sausage is browned and onion is tender. Add garlic; sauté 1 minute. Remove from heat. Stir in chicken and next 5 ingredients.
**2.** Bake at 350° for 20 minutes. Combine croutons and butter in a small bowl. Sprinkle over chicken mixture. Increase oven temperature to broil, and broil 1 to 2 minutes or until croutons are browned.

**Salt-and-Pepper Roast Turkey**

## SALT-AND-PEPPER ROAST TURKEY

**MAKES 8 TO 10 SERVINGS**
**HANDS-ON 20 MIN. TOTAL 4 HOURS, 25 MIN.**

*With a turkey this simple and with so few ingredients, focus on the techniques that matter most. First, pat the turkey very dry, which will help it achieve a crispier skin in the oven. Then season liberally with kosher salt. Season the cavity, gently under the skin, and again on the surface of the skin to enhance the flavor from the skin to the bone.*

1 (11- to 12-lb.) whole fresh turkey
⅓ cup canola oil, divided
2 Tbsp. kosher salt, divided
1 Tbsp. freshly ground black pepper, divided
Kitchen string

**1.** Preheat oven to 325°. Remove giblets and neck from turkey, and if desired, reserve for gravy. Rinse turkey with cold water; pat dry. Drain cavity well; pat dry. Loosen and lift skin from turkey breast with fingers (do not totally detach skin). Rub 2 Tbsp. oil, 2 tsp. salt, and 1 tsp. pepper on skin, under skin, and inside cavity.
**2.** Place turkey, breast side up, on a lightly greased roasting rack in a large roasting pan. Tie ends of legs together with kitchen string; tuck wing tips under. Brush turkey with remaining oil; sprinkle with remaining salt and pepper.
**3.** Bake at 325° for 3 hours and 45 minutes to 4 hours or until a meat thermometer inserted into thigh registers 165°. Let stand 20 minutes before carving.

## QUICK BEEF BOURGUIGNON

**MAKES 6 SERVINGS**
**HANDS-ON 26 MIN. TOTAL 26 MIN.**

*This dish achieves the rich, slow-simmered flavor of traditional beef bourguignon in minutes.*

1½ lb. beef tenderloin, cut into 1-inch pieces
½ tsp. table salt
¼ tsp. freshly ground black pepper
¼ cup butter, divided
2 cups frozen pearl onions, thawed and patted dry
1 (8-oz.) package fresh cremini mushrooms, quartered
2 cups sliced carrots
1 cup dry red wine
2 fresh thyme sprigs
1 (10½-oz.) can beef consommé
2 Tbsp. all-purpose flour
Garnish: fresh thyme leaves

**1.** Sprinkle tenderloin with salt and pepper. Melt 2 Tbsp. butter in a large skillet over medium-high heat. Brown beef in melted butter 5 minutes. Remove from skillet, and keep warm.
**2.** Melt remaining 2 Tbsp. butter in skillet. Add onions, mushrooms, and carrots; sauté 7 minutes or until mushrooms are browned. Add wine and thyme sprigs, and bring to a boil; reduce heat, and simmer 7 minutes or until wine is reduced by half, stirring to loosen browned bits from bottom of skillet.
**3.** Whisk together beef consommé and flour. Add to skillet with beef. Cook 3 minutes or until sauce thickens. Serve immediately.

## HERB-RUBBED VEAL CHOPS WITH PAN JUS

**MAKES 4 SERVINGS**
**HANDS-ON 25 MIN. TOTAL 45 MIN.**

1 Tbsp. coriander seeds
3 garlic cloves, minced
1 Tbsp. chopped fresh thyme
2 tsp. lemon zest
1 tsp. kosher salt
1 tsp. freshly ground black pepper
¼ cup vegetable oil, divided
4 (2½-inch-thick) veal chops (about 4 lb.)
1 shallot, finely chopped
1 cup dry white wine
1½ cups reduced-sodium fat-free chicken broth
½ cup heavy cream
3 Tbsp. cold butter, cut into pieces

**1.** Preheat oven to 450°. Place a small skillet over medium-high heat until hot; add coriander seeds, and cook, stirring constantly, 1 minute or until toasted. Cool completely. Crush toasted seeds.
**2.** Combine garlic, thyme, lemon zest, salt, pepper, 2 Tbsp. oil, and crushed coriander seeds in a small bowl. Rub veal chops with spice mixture.
**3.** Heat remaining 2 Tbsp. oil in a large ovenproof skillet over medium-high heat. Cook veal in hot oil 3 minutes or until browned. Turn and cook 1 more minute. Bake at 450° for 15 to 16 minutes or until desired degree of doneness. Remove veal from skillet, and keep warm, reserving drippings in skillet.
**4.** Sauté shallot in hot drippings over medium heat 5 minutes or until tender. Add white wine, and bring to a boil, stirring to loosen browned bits from bottom of skillet. Simmer 4 minutes or until liquid is reduced to ½ cup. Add chicken broth, and simmer 5 minutes or until liquid is reduced by half. Stir in cream. Bring to a boil, and cook 2 minutes. Remove from heat; gradually stir in butter and pan juices. Serve veal with sauce.

# Bars & Brownies

*Stop here if you crave irresistibly delightful goodies that are sure to please any crowd. Chocolate, toffee, marshmallow, and peppermint are just a few of the choices you'll find on these pages.*

## PEPPERMINT-MARSHMALLOW BROWNIES

**MAKES 16**
**HANDS-ON 10 MIN. TOTAL 2 HOURS, 20 MIN.**

*Dress up a premium brownie mix with a fluffy peppermint marshmallow frosting.*

1 (20-oz.) package dark chocolate brownie mix
½ cup vegetable oil
1 large egg
1 cup powdered sugar
½ cup butter, softened
3 Tbsp. marshmallow crème
¼ tsp. peppermint extract
¼ cup peppermint sparkling sugar
Crushed peppermint candy

**1.** Preheat oven to 325°. Prepare brownie mix batter according to package directions using oil and egg. Pour batter into a greased 9-inch pan.
**2.** Bake at 325° for 30 to 35 minutes or until a wooden pick inserted in center comes out with a few moist crumbs. Cool completely in pan on a wire rack (about 1 hour).
**3.** Beat powdered sugar and butter at medium speed with an electric mixer until light and fluffy. Beat in marshmallow crème and peppermint extract on low speed until blended. Spread frosting evenly over cooled brownies. Sprinkle with sparkling sugar and candy. Cut brownies into 16 squares.

**NOTE:** We tested with Betty Crocker Peppermint Sparkling Sugar.

## SALTED ENGLISH TOFFEE BROWNIES

**MAKES 16**
**HANDS-ON 8 MIN. TOTAL 1 HOUR, 48 MIN.**

*These fudge-style brownies are studded with toffee bits for a wholly decadent dessert.*

1 cup all-purpose flour
1⅓ cups granulated sugar
1 cup unsweetened cocoa
½ cup firmly packed brown sugar
¾ tsp. baking powder
¼ tsp. table salt
1 cup bittersweet chocolate chunks, divided
½ cup butter
2 large eggs, lightly beaten
1 tsp. vanilla extract
½ cup milk
1 (8-oz.) package toffee bits
¼ tsp. sea salt flakes
Sea salt

**1.** Preheat oven to 350°. Combine first 6 ingredients in a large bowl.
**2.** Microwave ½ cup chocolate chunks and butter in a microwave-safe bowl at HIGH 1 minute or until melted and smooth, stirring after 30 seconds. Gradually whisk in eggs and vanilla. Stir chocolate mixture into flour mixture. Stir in milk, remaining ½ cup chocolate chunks, and toffee bits.
**3.** Pour batter into a lightly greased 9-inch square pan. Sprinkle evenly with sea salt flakes.
**4.** Bake at 350° for 40 minutes or until a wooden pick inserted in center comes out with moist crumbs. Cool completely in pan on a wire rack (about 1 hour). Sprinkle with sea salt. Cut brownies into 16 squares.

## PEANUT BUTTER BROWNIES

**MAKES 2 DOZEN**
**HANDS-ON 19 MIN. TOTAL 1 HOUR, 54 MIN.**

*Peanut butter cups and peanut butter buttercream make these brownies a peanut butter lover's delight.*

1¼ cups butter, softened and divided
2 (4-oz.) semisweet chocolate baking bars, chopped
1 (4-oz.) unsweetened chocolate baking bar, chopped
2 cups granulated sugar
4 large eggs
1 cup all-purpose flour
1 tsp. vanilla extract
¼ tsp. table salt
1 (8-oz.) package peanut butter cup candy minis
¾ cup creamy peanut butter
1 cup powdered sugar
3 Tbsp. milk
Crushed peanut butter cups

**1.** Preheat oven to 350°. Line bottom and sides of a 13- x 9-inch pan with aluminum foil, allowing 2 to 3 inches to extend over sides; lightly grease foil.
**2.** Microwave 1 cup butter, semisweet chocolate, and unsweetened chocolate in a large microwave-safe bowl at HIGH 1½ to 2 minutes or until melted and smooth, stirring at 30-second intervals. Whisk in granulated sugar. Add eggs, 1 at a time, whisking just until blended after each addition. Whisk in flour, vanilla, and salt; fold in candy. Pour mixture into prepared pan.
**3.** Bake at 350° for 35 minutes or until a wooden pick inserted in center comes out with a few moist crumbs. Cool completely on a wire rack (about 1 hour).
**4.** Meanwhile, beat remaining ¼ cup butter and peanut butter at medium speed with an electric mixer until creamy; gradually add powdered sugar and milk, beating at low speed until blended. Spread over brownies.
**5.** Sprinkle with peanut butter cups. Lift brownies from pan, using foil sides as handles. Gently remove foil, and cut brownies into 24 squares.

## TRIPLE CHOCOLATE BROWNIES

**MAKES 20**
**HANDS-ON 12 MIN. TOTAL 2 HOURS, 27 MIN.**

1½ cups butter
5 oz. unsweetened chocolate, chopped
1 (12-oz.) bag semisweet chocolate morsels
1¾ cups sugar
1 Tbsp. vanilla extract
4 large eggs
1¾ cups all-purpose flour
2 tsp. baking powder
1 tsp. table salt
1½ cups milk chocolate morsels
Powdered sugar

**1.** Preheat oven to 350°. Line bottom and sides of a 13- x 9-inch pan with aluminum foil, allowing 2 to 3 inches to extend over sides; lightly grease foil.
**2.** Microwave butter, unsweetened chocolate, and 1 bag semisweet chocolate morsels in a large microwave-safe bowl at HIGH 1½ to 2 minutes or until melted and smooth, stirring at 30-second intervals. Whisk in sugar and vanilla. Add eggs, 1 at a time, whisking until blended after each addition. Whisk in flour, baking powder, and salt; fold in milk chocolate morsels. Pour into prepared pan.
**3.** Bake at 350° for 35 minutes or until a wooden pick inserted in center comes out with a few moist crumbs. Cool completely on a wire rack (about 1½ hours).
**4.** Sprinkle with powdered sugar. Lift brownies from pan, using foil sides as handles. Gently remove foil, and cut brownies into 20 squares.

## BOURBON-PECAN BLONDIES

**MAKES 32**
**HANDS-ON 10 MIN. TOTAL 1 HOUR, 40 MIN.**

*Brown sugar-laden, pecan-studded blondies get a boost from bourbon for a sweet Southern treat.*

- 1 cup butter, softened
- 2 cups firmly packed light brown sugar
- 2 large eggs
- ¼ cup bourbon
- 1½ tsp. vanilla extract
- 2 cups all-purpose flour
- 1 tsp. baking powder
- ½ tsp. table salt
- 1 cup white chocolate morsels
- 1 cup coarsely chopped toasted pecans

**1.** Preheat oven to 350°. Beat butter at medium speed with an electric mixer until creamy; gradually add brown sugar, beating well. Add eggs, 1 at a time, beating just until blended after each addition. Add bourbon and vanilla, beating until blended.

**2.** Combine flour, baking powder, and salt; gradually add to butter mixture, beating at low speed just until blended, stopping to scrape bowl as needed. Stir in white chocolate morsels and pecans. Pour batter into a lightly greased 13- x 9-inch pan.

**3.** Bake at 350° for 30 minutes or until a wooden pick inserted in center comes out clean. Cool completely in pan on a wire rack (about 1 hour). Cut into 32 squares.

## CARAMEL, MOCHA, ALMOND BROWNIES

**MAKES 16 SERVINGS**
**HANDS-ON 15 MIN. TOTAL 1 HOUR, 50 MIN.**

*Reminiscent of a favorite coffee shop drink, these brownies combine caramel and mocha-flavored almonds to make a standout dessert. If you can't find mocha-flavored almonds, use regular almonds and add 2 tsp. instant coffee to the batter.*

- 4 (1-oz.) unsweetened chocolate baking squares
- ¾ cup butter
- 1½ cups granulated sugar
- ½ cup firmly packed brown sugar
- 3 large eggs
- 1 cup all-purpose flour
- 1 tsp. vanilla extract
- ⅛ tsp. table salt
- 1 cup mocha-flavored almonds, chopped
- ½ cup chopped chocolate-covered caramels
- Powdered sugar

**1.** Preheat oven to 350°. Line bottom and sides of an 8-inch pan with aluminum foil, allowing 2 to 3 inches to extend over sides; lightly grease foil.

**2.** Microwave chocolate squares and butter in a large microwave-safe bowl at HIGH 1½ to 2 minutes or until melted and smooth, stirring at 30-second intervals. Whisk in granulated and brown sugars. Add eggs, 1 at a time, whisking just until blended after each addition. Whisk in flour, vanilla, and salt. Stir in almonds and caramel bits. Pour batter into prepared pan.

**3.** Bake at 350° for 35 to 40 minutes or until a wooden pick inserted in center comes out with a few moist crumbs. Cool completely on a wire rack (about 1 hour).

**4.** Dust brownies with powdered sugar. Lift brownies from pan, using foil sides as handles. Gently remove foil, and cut brownies into 16 squares.

# TIRAMISÙ BROWNIES

**MAKES 16**
**HANDS-ON 10 MIN. TOTAL 2 HOURS, 35 MIN.**

*These brownies are a decadent and rich treat for your holiday guests or gift giving.*

- ½ cup butter
- 6 oz. bittersweet baking chocolate, chopped
- 1½ cups granulated sugar
- 1 tsp. vanilla extract
- 3 large eggs
- ⅔ cup all-purpose flour
- ¼ cup plus 2 Tbsp. unsweetened cocoa, divided
- 1 tsp. instant espresso powder
- ⅛ tsp. table salt
- 5 Tbsp. coffee liqueur, divided
- 1 (8-oz.) container mascarpone cheese
- ⅓ cup powdered sugar
- 1 cup whipping cream

**1.** Preheat oven to 350°. Line bottom and sides of a 9-inch pan with aluminum foil, allowing 2 to 3 inches to extend over sides; lightly grease foil.
**2.** Microwave butter and chocolate in a medium microwave-safe bowl at HIGH 1 to 1½ minutes or until melted and smooth, stirring at 30-second intervals. Whisk in granulated sugar and vanilla. Add eggs, 1 at a time, whisking just until blended after each addition. Whisk in flour, ¼ cup cocoa, espresso powder, and salt.
**3.** Pour mixture into prepared pan.
**4.** Bake at 350° for 25 to 30 minutes or until a wooden pick inserted in center comes out with a few moist crumbs. Brush 2 Tbsp. coffee liqueur over brownies in pan. Cool completely on a wire rack (about 1 hour).
**5.** Beat mascarpone cheese and powdered sugar at low speed with an electric mixer until blended. Add whipping cream and remaining coffee liqueur; beat at medium speed until stiff peaks form (do not to overbeat). Spread over brownies in pan. Cover and chill 1 hour.
**6.** Dust brownies with remaining 2 Tbsp. cocoa. Lift brownies from pan, using foil sides as handles. Gently remove foil, and cut brownies into 16 squares.

# MACADAMIA TURTLE BARS

**MAKES 32**
**HANDS-ON 24 MIN. TOTAL 3 HOURS, 14 MIN.**

*Macadamia nuts replace the traditional pecans in this delightfully salty-sweet take on turtle candy.*

- 2 cups all-purpose flour
- ½ cup powdered sugar
- 1½ cups butter, divided
- 2 (6-oz.) jars dry-roasted macadamia nuts, coarsely chopped
- 1 cup firmly packed brown sugar
- ¾ cup heavy cream
- ½ cup light corn syrup
- 1 cup bittersweet chocolate morsels
- 1 Tbsp. shortening

**1.** Preheat oven to 350°. Line bottom and sides of a 13- x 9-inch pan with aluminum foil, allowing 2 to 3 inches to extend over sides; lightly grease foil.
**2.** Pulse flour and powdered sugar in a food processor 3 or 4 times or until combined. Cut 1 cup butter into small pieces; add to food processor. Pulse 10 times or until a crumbly dough forms. Press dough into bottom of prepared pan.
**3.** Bake at 350° for 20 minutes or until golden brown. Cool completely in pan on a wire rack (about 1 hour). Sprinkle macadamia nuts evenly over crust.
**4.** Bring brown sugar, heavy cream, corn syrup, and remaining ½ cup butter to a boil in a heavy medium saucepan over medium heat, and cook, stirring until sugar dissolves and butter is melted. Cook until a candy thermometer registers 240° (soft-ball stage), about 9 minutes. Do not stir. Remove from heat; pour over macadamia nuts in pan. Cool completely in pan on a wire rack (about 1 hour).
**5.** Microwave chocolate morsels and shortening in a small microwave-safe bowl at HIGH 1 minute or until melted and smooth, stirring at 30-second intervals. Drizzle chocolate over bars in pan. Refrigerate 30 minutes or until chocolate is firm.
**6.** Lift bars from pan, using foil sides as handles. Gently remove foil, and cut into 32 bars.

Share

# Savory Snacks

*December ushers in the season of giving. Here's a selection of bite-size treats that are sure to please everyone on your holiday list.*

# CARAMELIZED ONION-BACON JAM

**MAKES 5 (½-PT.) JARS**
**HANDS-ON 27 MIN.   TOTAL 1 HOUR, 15 MIN.**

*This versatile jam can be served as a condiment with chicken or pork, or used as an appetizer spooned over cream cheese and served with crackers.*

- 10 bacon slices
- 2 large red onions, halved and vertically sliced
- 2 large sweet onions, halved and vertically sliced
- 2 large shallots, halved and vertically sliced
- ½ cup firmly packed light brown sugar
- ½ cup apple cider vinegar
- ½ cup apple cider
- 1 Tbsp. chopped fresh thyme
- 1 tsp. table salt

**1.** Cook bacon in a Dutch oven over medium-high heat 8 to 10 minutes or until crisp; remove bacon, and drain on paper towels, reserving drippings in Dutch oven. Crumble bacon.
**2.** Reduce heat to medium-low. Sauté onions and shallots in hot drippings 15 minutes or until golden brown and tender, stirring occasionally. Add brown sugar and next 4 ingredients. Cook over low heat 40 minutes or until thickened, stirring occasionally. Remove from heat; stir in bacon. Cool to room temperature. Store, covered, in refrigerator.

# THREE-OLIVE TAPENADE

**MAKES 16 SERVINGS**
**HANDS-ON 6 MIN. TOTAL 6 MIN.**

*Tapenade makes a fabulous appetizer when spread on crusty bread or hearty crackers, or use it as a sandwich condiment or a topping for grilled chicken or fish.*

1 cup pitted kalamata olives
½ cup pimiento-stuffed Spanish olives
½ cup pitted oil-cured olives
3 garlic cloves
2 anchovy fillets
½ cup olive oil
2 Tbsp. drained capers
1 Tbsp. lemon juice
2 Tbsp. torn fresh basil leaves
2 tsp. fresh thyme leaves
½ tsp. freshly ground black pepper

**1.** Pulse all ingredients in a food processor 10 to 12 times or until finely chopped. Store in an airtight container in refrigerator for up to 1 week. Serve cold or at room temperature.

## HAVARTI-DILL COINS

**MAKES 12 DOZEN**
**HANDS-ON 25 MIN. TOTAL 2 HOURS, 55 MIN.**

*These savory treats are perfect for your next holiday hostess gift.*

- 1½ cups shredded Havarti cheese with dill
- ¾ cup all-purpose flour
- ¼ cup butter, cut into small pieces
- ½ tsp. kosher salt
- 1 Tbsp. half-and-half
- 1 Tbsp. melted butter
- 1 Tbsp. chopped fresh dill

**1.** Preheat oven to 350°. Pulse first 4 ingredients 10 to 12 times until mixture resembles coarse crumbs. Add half-and-half; process 10 seconds or until dough forms a ball.
**2.** Place dough on a floured surface, and roll dough to ⅛-inch thickness. Cut with a 1-inch round cutter; place 1 inch apart on ungreased baking sheets. Brush with melted butter; sprinkle with dill.
**3.** Bake at 350° for 20 minutes or until edges are lightly browned. Cool on baking sheets 30 minutes. Transfer to wire racks, and cool completely.

## PARMESAN CRISPS

**MAKES 3 DOZEN**
**HANDS-ON 12 MIN. TOTAL 56 MIN.**

*Spiced Parmesan wafers, packed with intense flavor, are a great stand-alone as a savory snack or as an accompaniment with salads. Parmigiano-Reggiano cheese is recommended for the best flavor and texture; however Parmesan cheese can be substituted in a pinch.*

2 cups (8 oz.) freshly grated Parmigiano-Reggiano cheese
Parchment paper
¼ tsp. garlic powder
¼ tsp. smoked paprika
⅛ tsp. ground red pepper

**1.** Preheat oven to 400°. Spoon cheese by tablespoonfuls 3 inches apart onto 2 lightly greased parchment paper-lined baking sheets. Gently press cheese with the back of a spoon or fingers to flatten.
**2.** Combine garlic powder and remaining 2 ingredients in a small bowl. Sprinkle evenly over cheese.
**3.** Bake at 400° for 7 to 8 minutes or until golden brown. Cool completely on pans on wire racks. Use a flat spatula to remove from parchment paper. Store between layers of parchment paper in an airtight container at room temperature for up to 1 week.

## ROSEMARY-GORGONZOLA CHEESE WAFERS

**MAKES 4 DOZEN**
**HANDS-ON 10 MIN. TOTAL 2 HOURS, 42 MIN.**

*Store tightly wrapped dough logs in the refrigerator for up to four days.*

½ cup butter, softened
6 oz. Gorgonzola cheese, softened
1 Tbsp. chopped fresh rosemary
½ tsp. freshly ground black pepper
¼ tsp. table salt
1½ cups all-purpose flour
½ cup chopped pecans

**1.** Beat butter and cheese at medium speed with an electric mixer 2 minutes or until creamy. Add rosemary, pepper, and salt, beating until combined. Gradually add flour, beating 1 minute or until crumbly. Add 1 Tbsp. water, beating at low speed just until dough forms; beat in pecans.
**2.** Divide dough in half; shape each portion into a 6-inch log. Wrap each log in plastic wrap; chill 1 hour or until firm.
**3.** Preheat oven to 350°. Cut dough into ¼-inch slices. Place on ungreased baking sheets.
**4.** Bake at 350° for 12 to 14 minutes or until golden brown. Cool on pans 2 minutes; transfer to wire racks, and cool completely (about 30 minutes).

Spicy Barbecue Snack Mix

Honey-Rosemary Cashews

## SPICY BARBECUE SNACK MIX

**MAKES 12 CUPS**
**HANDS-ON 10 MIN. TOTAL 1 HOUR, 40 MIN.**

*In honor of the South we just had to tweak the traditional snack and add a bold BBQ twist.*

2 cups habanero barbecue-flavored almonds
2 cups rice cereal squares
2 cups corn cereal squares
1½ cups hot and spicy bite-size Cheddar cheese crackers
1½ cups jalapeño pretzel pieces
3 cups mesquite barbecue-seasoned kettle-cooked potato chips
½ cup butter, melted
3 Tbsp. Worcestershire sauce
1½ tsp. garlic salt
¾ tsp. onion powder

**1.** Preheat oven to 250°. Combine almonds, cereal, crackers, pretzels, and chips in a large roasting pan.
**2.** Combine butter, Worcestershire sauce, garlic salt, and onion powder in a medium bowl until well blended. Drizzle over mixture in pan; toss gently to coat.
**3.** Bake at 250° for 1 hour, stirring every 15 minutes. Cool in pans 30 minutes. Store in an airtight container.

## HONEY-ROSEMARY CASHEWS

**MAKES 4 CUPS**
**HANDS-ON 3 MIN. TOTAL 45 MIN.**

*Sweet and salty, savory and citrusy...these crunchy treats cover all your snack food needs.*

¼ cup butter
4 cups raw cashews
1 Tbsp. orange zest
2 Tbsp. honey
Parchment paper
2 tsp. kosher salt
1 Tbsp. finely chopped fresh rosemary

**1.** Preheat oven to 350°. Cook butter in a medium-size heavy saucepan over medium heat, stirring constantly, 3 to 5 minutes or just until butter begins to turn golden brown. Immediately remove pan from heat, and stir in cashews, orange zest, and honey. Pour cashew mixture in a single layer on a rimmed baking sheet lined with parchment paper. Sprinkle with salt.
**2.** Bake at 350° for 9 minutes or until toasted and fragrant, stirring after 6 minutes; sprinkle with rosemary. Bake 3 more minutes. Cool completely on pan (about 30 minutes). Store in an airtight container.

## COCONUT CURRY POPCORN

**MAKES 9 SERVINGS**
**HANDS-ON 9 MIN. TOTAL 9 MIN.**

*To spice up this ethnic snack, use Madras curry powder that has a bit of heat.*

2 Tbsp. canola oil
2 tsp. curry powder
¼ cup popcorn kernels, unpopped
¼ cup butter, melted
¼ tsp. table salt
1 cup toasted unsweetened organic flaked coconut
1½ cups roasted, salted cashews

**1.** Heat oil in Dutch oven over medium-high heat; add curry powder, and cook 1 minute. Add popcorn kernels; cover and cook 4 minutes or until popcorn is popped, shaking pan constantly.
**2.** Transfer popcorn to a large bowl. Add butter, salt, coconut, and cashews; toss well to combine.

## GOLD DUSTED WHITE CHOCOLATE POPCORN

**MAKES 9 SERVINGS**
**HANDS-ON 10 MIN. TOTAL 25 MIN.**

1 (3.3-oz.) bag butter-flavored microwave popcorn, popped
1 cup salted mixed nuts
1 cup dried cranberries
1 (12-oz.) package white chocolate morsels
½ tsp. ground cinnamon
Edible gold dust

**1.** Place popcorn in a large bowl, discarding unpopped kernels. Stir in nuts and cranberries.
**2.** Microwave white chocolate morsels in a 2-cup glass measuring cup at HIGH 1½ minutes or until melted and smooth, stirring at 30-second intervals. Pour over popcorn mixture, stirring until evenly coated.
**3.** Spread mixture in a single layer in a 15- x 10-inch jelly-roll pan. Sprinkle evenly with cinnamon. Let stand 15 minutes or until chocolate hardens. Sprinkle with gold dust. Break into pieces; serve immediately, or store in an airtight container up to 3 days.

## THYME-BROWN BUTTER NUT MIX

**MAKES 8½ CUPS**
**HANDS-ON 3 MIN. TOTAL 43 MIN.**

*Have this nut mix on hand for a quick and simple snack as holiday visitors come and go.*

2 cups toasted pecan halves
2 cups toasted whole almonds
2 cups toasted cashews
2 cups toasted walnut halves
¼ cup butter
3 Tbsp. maple syrup
1 Tbsp. fresh thyme leaves
1½ tsp. table salt
1½ tsp. chili powder
½ tsp. freshly ground black pepper
¼ tsp. ground red pepper

**1.** Preheat oven to 350°. Place nuts on a large rimmed baking sheet.
**2.** Cook butter in a small heavy saucepan over medium heat, stirring constantly, 3 minutes or just until butter begins to turn golden brown. Immediately remove pan from heat, and stir in maple syrup and next 5 ingredients. Pour mixture over nuts on pan; toss to coat.
**3.** Bake at 350° for 10 minutes or until toasted and almost dry. Cool completely in pan on a wire rack (about 30 minutes).

Coconut Curry Popcorn

Thyme-Brown Butter Nut Mix

# Sweet Inspiration

*Delight friends and family with some irresistible treats this holiday season. Pull it all together using some of our creative packaging ideas.*

# COCONUT ALMOND TRUFFLES

**MAKES 16**
**HANDS-ON 23 MIN. TOTAL 38 MIN.**

*Semisweet chocolate instead of bittersweet can also be used to coat these truffles if you desire a sweeter flavor.*

1 (8-oz.) can almond paste
¾ cup sweetened flaked coconut, toasted and divided
½ cup chopped almonds
¼ tsp. coconut extract
2 (4-oz.) bittersweet chocolate baking bars
1 Tbsp. shortening
Parchment paper

**1.** Pulse almond paste, ½ cup flaked coconut, almonds, and coconut extract in a food processor 3 or 4 times or until combined. (Mixture will be crumbly.) Shape dough into 16 (1-inch) balls.
**2.** Microwave chocolate and shortening in a 4-cup glass measuring cup at HIGH 1½ to 2 minutes or until melted and smooth, stirring at 30-second intervals. Dip balls into chocolate. Place on a parchment paper-lined baking sheet. Immediately sprinkle tops with remaining ¼ cup flaked coconut. Chill until firm. Store in an airtight container in refrigerator up to 2 weeks.

## Foolproof Fudge

**Gather all the equipment and ingredients** that you'll need before you begin to prepare the recipe. That way you won't have to stop in the middle of making the fudge and risk messing up the recipe.

**Be sure to line the pan** with greased parchment paper before you begin. That means you can pour the hot mixture directly into the pan and makes removing the fudge much easier after it's cooled.

**When the fudge has cooled** remove it from the pan onto a cutting board, and cut it into pieces using a sharp knife.

# BOOZY CARAMEL FUDGE

**MAKES 16 SERVINGS**
**HANDS-ON 25 MIN. TOTAL 2 HOURS, 25 MIN.**

Parchment paper
¾ cup sugar
1 Tbsp. fresh lemon juice
⅓ cup heavy cream
2 Tbsp. butter
2 (14-oz.) cans sweetened condensed milk
2 (12-oz.) packages semisweet chocolate morsels
¼ cup dark rum
2½ Tbsp. butter
¼ tsp. table salt

**1.** Line a 9-inch square pan with parchment paper; grease paper. Bring sugar, ¼ cup water, and lemon juice to a boil in a small saucepan over medium-high heat. Boil 8 to 10 minutes or until sugar begins to brown. (Do not stir.) Stir in cream and 2 Tbsp. butter; remove from heat. Let stand, stirring constantly, until no longer bubbling.
**2.** Microwave sweetened condensed milk and semisweet chocolate morsels in a large microwave-safe bowl at HIGH 3 minutes, stirring at 1-minute intervals. Stir in rum, 2½ Tbsp. butter, and salt. Immediately pour into prepared pan. Immediately pour caramel over chocolate mixture; gently swirl with a knife. Chill 2 to 4 hours. Cut into pieces; wrap in parchment paper. Store in refrigerator up to 1 week. Let stand at room temperature 15 minutes before serving.

Boozy Caramel Fudge
Merry Christmas
Coconut Almond Truffles

Bacon-Pecan Shortbread

Double-Chocolate Espresso Cookies

# DOUBLE-CHOCOLATE ESPRESSO COOKIES

**MAKES 3½ DOZEN**
**HANDS-ON 10 MIN. TOTAL 2 HOURS, 26 MIN.**

*Store a batch of this decadent chocolate cookie dough in the freezer to have on hand, and bake as needed for any last-minute holiday gifts. To easily scoop the dough, use a 1½-inch-diameter ice cream scoop.*

1¼ cups butter, softened
1 cup granulated sugar
¾ cup firmly packed brown sugar
2 large eggs
2 tsp. instant espresso powder
1 tsp. vanilla extract
2¼ cups all-purpose flour
⅔ cup Dutch process dark cocoa
1 tsp. baking soda
½ tsp. table salt
¾ cup dark chocolate-covered espresso beans
2 (4-oz.) white chocolate baking bars, chopped
Parchment paper

**1.** Preheat oven to 350°. Beat butter and sugars at medium speed with an electric mixer until light and fluffy. Add eggs, 1 at a time, beating until blended after each addition. Beat in espresso powder and vanilla.
**2.** Combine flour and next 3 ingredients in a medium bowl; gradually add to butter mixture, beating until blended. Stir in espresso beans and white chocolate.
**3.** Drop dough by heaping tablespoonfuls 2 inches apart onto parchment paper-lined baking sheets.
**4.** Bake at 350° for 12 to 14 minutes or until set. Cool on baking sheets 2 minutes. Transfer to wire racks, and cool completely (about 20 minutes).

# BACON-PECAN SHORTBREAD

**MAKES 2 DOZEN**
**HANDS-ON 12 MIN. TOTAL 1 HOUR, 52 MIN.**

*Great for holiday gift giving, these buttery, savory shortbread cookies are delicious alone or drizzled with Maple Glaze for an over-the-top experience.*

1 cup butter, softened
¾ cup powdered sugar
¼ cup granulated sugar
½ tsp. vanilla extract
2 cups all-purpose flour
⅓ cup cornstarch
¼ tsp. table salt
8 cooked bacon slices, crumbled (¾ cup)
1 cup chopped pecans, toasted
Maple Glaze

**1.** Preheat oven to 350°. Line bottom and sides of a 13- x 9-inch pan with aluminum foil, allowing 2 to 3 inches to extend over sides; lightly grease foil.
**2.** Beat butter and sugars at medium speed with a heavy-duty electric stand mixer until light and fluffy. Beat in vanilla.
**3.** Whisk together flour, cornstarch, and salt; add to butter mixture, and beat until dough just comes together. Gently stir in crumbled bacon and pecans. Press dough evenly into prepared pan. Refrigerate for 10 minutes or until firm.
**4.** Bake at 350° for 25 to 30 minutes or until golden. Cool completely on a wire rack (about 1 hour). Lift shortbread from pan, using foil sides as handles. Gently remove foil, and cut shortbread into 24 rectangles. Drizzle shortbread with Maple Glaze.

## MAPLE GLAZE

**MAKES ⅔ CUP**
**HANDS-ON 3 MIN. TOTAL 3 MIN.**

**1.** Whisk together 1¼ cups powdered sugar, ¼ tsp. maple extract, and 1½ Tbsp. milk until smooth, adding additional milk for desired consistency.

## RED VELVET MOON PIES

**MAKES 18 MOON PIES**
**HANDS-ON 30 MIN. TOTAL 1 HOUR**

2¾ cups all-purpose flour
⅓ cup unsweetened cocoa
1½ tsp. baking powder
½ tsp. baking soda
¼ tsp. table salt
1 cup butter, softened
1¼ cups sugar
2 large eggs
2 Tbsp. red liquid food coloring
1 Tbsp. vanilla extract
¾ cup buttermilk
Parchment paper
Marshmallow Filling

**1.** Preheat oven to 350°. Combine first 5 ingredients in a medium bowl.
**2.** Beat butter at medium speed with an electric mixer 2 minutes or until creamy. Gradually add sugar, beating well. Add eggs, 1 at a time, beating until blended after each addition. Beat in food coloring and vanilla.
**3.** Add flour mixture alternately with buttermilk, beginning and ending with flour mixture. Beat at low speed until blended after each addition, stopping to scrape bowl as needed.
**4.** Drop dough by tablespoonfuls onto parchment paper-lined baking sheets. Spread dough to 2-inch rounds.
**5.** Bake at 350° for 15 minutes or until tops are set. Cool on baking sheets 5 minutes. Remove to wire racks, and cool completely (about 20 minutes). Spread filling onto each cookie. Top with cookie, flat side down.

## MARSHMALLOW FILLING

**MAKES ABOUT 1½ CUPS**
**HANDS-ON 5 MIN. TOTAL 5 MIN.**

½ cup butter, softened
1 cup sifted powdered sugar
1 cup marshmallow crème
½ tsp. vanilla extract

**1.** Beat butter at medium speed with an electric mixer until creamy; gradually add sugar, beating well. Add remaining ingredients, beating until well blended.

## TROPICAL WHITE CHOCOLATE FUDGE

**MAKES 16 SERVINGS**
**HANDS-ON 21 MIN. TOTAL 2 HOURS, 21 MIN.**

*Treat your guests to a taste of the tropics with this fruit- and nut-studded confection, or give as a gift for fans of fudge with a twist.*

½ cup butter
2 cups sugar
¾ cup sour cream
3 (4-oz.) white chocolate baking bars, chopped
1 (7-oz.) jar marshmallow crème
½ cup dried apricots, chopped
½ cup dried pineapple, chopped
¾ cup chopped macadamia nuts
½ cup toasted sweetened shredded coconut

**1.** Line bottom and sides of a 9-inch square pan with aluminum foil, allowing 2 to 3 inches to extend over sides; lightly grease foil.
**2.** Combine butter, sugar, and sour cream in a large heavy saucepan over medium heat. Bring to a boil; cook, stirring constantly, until a candy thermometer registers 234° (soft ball stage), about 5 minutes.
**3.** Remove from heat; stir in chocolate and marshmallow crème until melted. Fold in dried fruit and nuts; quickly pour into prepared pan, spreading evenly. Sprinkle coconut over top, pressing gently. Cool completely in pan (about 2 hours). Lift fudge from pan, using foil sides as handles. Gently remove foil, and cut fudge into 64 squares.

**Red Velvet Moon Pies**

**Tropical White Chocolate Fudge**

# WALNUT BUTTER CRUNCH TOFFEE

**MAKES 2¼ LB.**
**HANDS-ON 31 MIN. TOTAL 1 HOUR, 47 MIN.**

*Impress your friends and family with this super-decadent yet easy-to-make treat.*

- 1½ cups toasted chopped walnuts, divided
- 1¾ cups firmly packed brown sugar
- 1 cup plus 2 Tbsp. butter
- 1½ Tbsp. light corn syrup
- 1 tsp. vanilla extract
- 1½ cups semisweet chocolate morsels

**1.** Spread walnuts in a single layer on a jelly-roll pan coated with cooking spray.
**2.** Bring brown sugar, butter, corn syrup, and ⅓ cup water to a boil in a medium-size heavy saucepan over medium heat, stirring until sugar dissolves. Cook until mixture is golden brown and candy thermometer registers 290° to 310°, about 15 minutes. Remove from heat; stir in vanilla. Immediately pour over walnuts on baking sheet.
**3.** Sprinkle chocolate morsels over sugar mixture; let stand 1 minute. Spread melted chocolate over top with a spatula. Chill 1 hour. Break into pieces.

# HAZELNUT AND BROWN BUTTER BISCOTTI

**MAKES 2 DOZEN**
**HANDS-ON 18 MIN. TOTAL 2 HOURS, 48 MIN.**

*Personalize these tasty biscotti with your choice of powdered sugar, chocolate drizzle, or half chocolate dunk—or a combination of all three for variety.*

- ½ cup butter
- 1 cup granulated sugar
- 2 large eggs
- 2 Tbsp. hazelnut liqueur
- 2½ cups all-purpose flour
- 1½ tsp. baking powder
- ¼ tsp. table salt
- 8 oz. (1½ cups) blanched hazelnuts, chopped and toasted
- ½ cup powdered sugar

**1.** Preheat oven to 350°. Cook butter in a 2-qt. heavy saucepan over medium heat, stirring constantly, 6 to 8 minutes or just until butter begins to turn golden brown. Immediately remove pan from heat, and pour butter into a medium bowl. (Butter will continue to darken if left in saucepan.) Let stand 20 minutes or until room temperature.
**2.** Beat cooled butter, granulated sugar, eggs, and liqueur at medium speed with an electric mixer until creamy.
**3.** Combine flour, baking powder, and salt; add to butter mixture, beating at low speed just until blended. Stir in hazelnuts.
**4.** Divide dough in half. Lightly flour hands, and shape each portion into a 9- x 2-inch slightly flattened log on a lightly greased baking sheet.
**5.** Bake at 350° for 30 minutes or until golden brown. Cool on pan 5 minutes; transfer to a wire rack, and cool completely (about 1 hour).
**6.** Cut each log diagonally into ¾-inch-thick slices with a serrated knife, using a gentle sawing motion; place slices on ungreased baking sheets.
**7.** Bake at 350° for 8 minutes; turn cookies over, and bake 15 to 20 more minutes. Remove to wire racks, and cool completely (about 30 minutes). Dust with powdered sugar.

**NOTE:** We tested with Frangelico liqueur.

**Walnut Butter Crunch Toffee**

**Hazelnut and Brown Butter Biscotti**

Raspberry Marshmallows

# RASPBERRY MARSHMALLOWS

**MAKES ABOUT 4½ DOZEN**
**HANDS-ON 31 MIN. TOTAL 12 HOURS, 36 MIN.**

*These raspberry-flavored marshmallows are delicious in hot chocolate as they are, or drizzled with melted bittersweet chocolate before packaging for an even more swoon-worthy sweet. Cut into shapes using lightly greased small cookie cutters, if desired, and reserve any scraps for your own cup of cocoa.*

¾ cup fresh raspberries
½ cup plus 2 Tbsp. powdered sugar
1 cup cold water, divided
3 envelopes unflavored gelatin
2 cups granulated sugar
⅔ cup light corn syrup
¼ tsp. table salt
1 tsp. vanilla extract
½ cup cornstarch

**1.** Line bottom and sides of a 13- x 9-inch pan with aluminum foil, allowing 2 to 3 inches to extend over sides; lightly grease foil.
**2.** Process raspberries and 2 Tbsp. powdered sugar in a blender or food processor until smooth, stopping to scrap down sides as needed. Pour raspberry mixture through a wire-mesh strainer into a bowl using the back of a spoon to squeeze out juice. Discard pulp and seeds.
**3.** Place ½ cup cold water in bowl of a heavy-duty electric stand mixer fitted with whisk attachment. Sprinkle gelatin over water; let stand 5 minutes.
**4.** Combine granulated sugar, corn syrup, salt, and remaining ½ cup cold water in a medium saucepan. Bring to a boil over medium heat, stirring occasionally until sugar dissolves. Cook, without stirring, until a candy thermometer registers 240°, about 6 minutes. Remove from heat.
**5.** With mixer on low speed, slowly pour hot syrup in a thin stream over gelatin mixture. Increase speed to medium-high, and beat until very thick and stiff, about 8 minutes. Beat in raspberry puree and vanilla. Quickly pour marshmallow mixture into prepared pan, smoothing top with a lightly greased spatula.
**6.** Combine remaining ½ cup powdered sugar and cornstarch in a small bowl. Dust top of marshmallow mixture in pan with about ⅓ cup powdered sugar mixture. Let marshmallows stand, uncovered, 12 hours or overnight.
**7.** Lift marshmallows from pan using foil sides as handles; flip over onto a cutting board. Gently remove foil. Dust marshmallows with ⅓ cup powdered sugar mixture. Cut into 1½-inch squares using a lightly greased knife. Dust cut sides of marshmallows with remaining powdered sugar mixture, shaking off excess.

# BLUEBERRY-POMEGRANATE FRUIT JELLIES

**MAKES ABOUT 5 DOZEN**
**HANDS-ON 21 MIN. TOTAL 2 HOURS, 46 MIN.**

*Try these jellies with different combinations of fruit juices and jams or preserves, such as peach nectar and apricot preserves, or cranberry juice and grape jam.*

1⅓ cups blueberry-pomegranate juice, divided
5 envelopes unflavored gelatin
2½ cups sugar, divided
1 (18-oz.) jar blueberry preserves

**1.** Line bottom and sides of an 8-inch square pan with plastic wrap, allowing 2 to 3 inches to extend over sides; lightly grease plastic wrap.
**2.** Place ⅔ cup pomegranate juice in a small bowl. Sprinkle gelatin over juice; let stand 5 minutes.
**3.** Bring remaining ⅔ cup pomegranate juice and 1½ cups sugar to a boil in a medium saucepan over medium-high heat. Boil, stirring constantly, 3 minutes or until sugar is dissolved. Whisk in blueberry preserves; return to a boil, and cook 2 minutes or until thick and syrupy. Remove from heat; add gelatin mixture, whisking until gelatin is dissolved.
**4.** Pour mixture through a fine wire-mesh strainer into a medium bowl; cool 20 minutes. Pour into prepared pan. Refrigerate, uncovered, 2 hours or until set.
**5.** Place remaining 1 cup sugar in a small bowl. Turn jellies out onto a cutting board; carefully remove plastic wrap. Cut into 1-inch squares; toss in sugar to coat.

# Something Extra

*Spread holiday cheer with ingredients to make party-perfect drinks. Present them in pretty glass jars or other packaging for festive gifts.*

# VANILLA GINGER SYRUP

**MAKES 3 CUPS**
**HANDS-ON 5 MIN. TOTAL 1 HOUR, 28 MIN.**

*Add this delicious ginger syrup to your next martini for a warm twist. Or, it's equally indulgent served over pound cake, fruit, or ice cream.*

- ½ vanilla bean
- 1 (3-inch) lemon peel strip
- 1 cup (5 oz.) peeled and thinly sliced fresh ginger
- 2 cups sugar
- 1 (3-inch) cinnamon stick

**1.** Split vanilla bean lengthwise. Combine vanilla bean, next 4 ingredients, and 2 cups water in a 2-qt. saucepan; bring to a boil. Reduce heat, and simmer, partially covered, 20 minutes. Cool completely, about 30 to 40 minutes. Pour mixture through a wire-mesh strainer, reserving vanilla bean. Scrape seeds from vanilla bean into syrup; discard vanilla pod. Cover and refrigerate for up to 3 weeks.

# DRUNKEN CHERRIES

**MAKES 1 (1-PT.) JAR**
**HANDS-ON 5 MIN. TOTAL 5 MIN., PLUS 3 WEEKS STORAGE**

*Not only do these vanilla-infused bourbon cherries make a great addition to cocktails but they're also good over ice cream and pound cake.*

- 1 (12-oz.) package frozen dark cherries, thawed and drained
- 1 vanilla bean
- ⅓ cup bourbon
- ¼ cup sugar

**1.** Pack cherries and vanilla bean in a 1-pt. canning jar. Combine bourbon and sugar in a 2-cup glass measuring cup, stirring until sugar is dissolved. Pour bourbon mixture over cherries until completely covered, filling to ½ inch from top; seal and refrigerate at least 3 weeks, shaking jar once a day.

# SPICED PEAR LIQUEUR

**MAKES 4 (1-PT.) JARS    HANDS-ON 12 MIN.**
**TOTAL 1 HOUR, 15 MIN., PLUS 4 WEEKS STORAGE**

*This sweet liqueur can be served on its own or mixed with your favorite whiskey or bitters.*

1 lemon
6 ripe pears, peeled and sliced (about 6 cups)
3 cups sugar
1 (2-inch) piece fresh ginger, peeled and sliced
2 cups brandy

**1.** Peel lemon using a vegetable peeler. Scrape white pith from lemon rind strips; discard pith. Divide pears and lemon peel evenly between 4 (1-pt.) clean jars.

**2.** Bring sugar, 3 cups water, and ginger to a boil in a medium saucepan over medium heat. Reduce heat to low, and simmer, stirring constantly, until sugar dissolves. Remove from heat; let stand 15 minutes.

**3.** Pour 1¼ cups sugar mixture through a fine wire-mesh strainer into a measuring cup, discarding ginger. (Refrigerate remaining syrup in an airtight container for up to 2 weeks.) Pour sugar mixture evenly over pears and lemon peel. Pour brandy evenly into jars until filled; seal tightly. Shake to combine. Store in a cool, dark place for 4 weeks, shaking jars every few days.

**4.** Pour infused brandy through a fine wire-mesh strainer lined with 3 layers of cheesecloth or a coffee filter into clean jars. Store at room temperature for up to 6 months.

# RHUBARB LIQUEUR

**MAKES 2 (1-QT.) JARS**
**HANDS-ON 10 MIN. TOTAL 1 HOUR, 40 MIN., PLUS 4 WEEKS**

*The sweet-tart combination of this vanilla-flecked rhubarb liqueur is a refreshing addition to cocktails but is equally delicious served chilled, straight up.*

2 lb. fresh rhubarb, chopped, or frozen rhubarb, thawed (about 5 cups)
1 (750-milliliter) bottle vodka
2 cups sugar
1 vanilla bean

**1.** Combine rhubarb and vodka in a 1-gal. glass jar with a lid. Cover and let stand at room temperature in a cool, dark place 3 to 4 weeks or until rhubarb loses its color.
**2.** Bring sugar and 2 cups water to a boil in a large saucepan over medium-high heat. Boil, stirring constantly, 2 to 3 minutes or until sugar is dissolved and mixture is clear. Split vanilla bean lengthwise. Scrape seeds from vanilla bean into sugar syrup; add vanilla bean. Cool 1½ hours or to room temperature. Remove vanilla bean.
**3.** Strain rhubarb mixture through a fine wire-mesh strainer lined with 3 layers of dampened cheesecloth or 1 coffee filter into sugar syrup in saucepan, stirring to combine; discard rhubarb.
**4.** Pour mixture into 2 (1-qt.) clean glass jars. Seal, label, and store in refrigerator.

# POMEGRANATE-CITRUS-INFUSED VODKA

**MAKES 1¾ CUPS**
**HANDS-ON 10 MIN. TOTAL 48 HOURS, 10 MIN.**

*Use this citrusy infusion as a basis for a martini or spiked cider. It's perfect for using up all the leftover fruit that comes as a gift in a fruit basket.*

1½ cups ruby red grapefruit-flavored vodka
2 (4.3-oz) packages pomegranate seeds
1 cup ruby red grapefruit sections (1 grapefruit)
1 cup kumquats, halved
2 star anise

**1.** Pour vodka into a clean 1-qt. jar. Add pomegranate seeds, grapefruit, kumquats, and star anise. Cover and refrigerate 2 days and up to 1 week. Pour mixture through a fine wire-mesh strainer before using.

# POMEGRANATE-CITRUS MARTINI

**1.** Combine 3 Tbsp. Pomegranate-Citrus-Infused Vodka, 1 Tbsp. Campari, 1 Tbsp. fresh lemon ginger, and 1 Tbsp. ginger simple syrup in a cocktail shaker. Add ice cubes; cover with lid, and shake vigorously until thoroughly chilled (about 30 seconds). Strain into a chilled martini glass.

Pomegranate-Citrus-Infused Vodka

Rhubarb Liqueur

## WARMING SPICE BITTERS

**MAKES 1 (1-PT.) JAR**
**HANDS-ON 5 MIN. TOTAL 3 WEEKS, 5 MIN.**

*Warming Spice Bitters add a depth of spiciness and flavor to both hot and cold beverages. It's also great for winter cocktails.*

1 orange
1 vanilla bean
2 Tbsp. chopped dried orange peel
6 cardamom pods, crushed
1 (2-inch) piece fresh ginger, peeled and coarsely chopped
3 star anise
½ tsp. organic wild cherry bark
½ tsp. cassia chips
½ tsp. gentian root
¼ tsp. whole allspice
¼ tsp. whole cloves
2 cups high-proof rye whiskey
3 Tbsp. agave syrup

**1.** Peel orange using a vegetable peeler. Scrape white pith from orange rind strips; discard pith. (Reserve orange flesh for another use.) Split vanilla bean lengthwise. Scrape seeds from vanilla bean into a clean 1-qt. glass jar with a lid. Place vanilla bean pod, fresh orange peel, dried orange peel, and next 8 ingredients in jar; pour whiskey over mixture, adding more if necessary to cover. Cover and let stand at room temperature 2 weeks, shaking the jar once a day.
**2.** Pour mixture through a fine wire-mesh strainer lined with 3 layers of cheesecloth into a large bowl. Squeeze cheesecloth over the bowl to squeeze out excess liquid. Wash jar; return mixture to clean, dry jar. Add agave syrup; cover with lid and shake well. Cover and let stand at room temperature 3 days.
**3.** Pour into jars or bottles. Seal, label, and store at room temperature up to 1 year.

## THE ETERNAL OPTIMIST

**1.** Combine 1½ oz. rye whiskey, 4 drops Warming Spice Bitters, ½ oz. vermouth, ½ oz. ginger simple syrup, and ½ oz. fresh orange juice in a cocktail shaker. Add ice cubes; cover with lid, and shake vigorously until thoroughly chilled (about 30 seconds). Strain into a rocks glass filled with ice cubes. Garnish with an orange twist.

**NOTE:** We tested with 100-proof Colonel E.H. Taylor Straight Rye Whiskey. Cassia chips can be found at health food stores or ordered online.

# THANKS TO THESE **CONTRIBUTORS**


## *Thanks to the following businesses*

Anthropologie

Architectural Heritage

At Home

Attic Antiques

Bromberg's

Carousel Tack Shoppe

Chelsea Antiques Mall

Crate & Barrel

Collier's Nursery

Davis Wholesale Florist

Flowerbuds

Greystone Antiques

Hanna Antiques

Henhouse Antiques

Hobby Lobby

Lamb's Ears Ltd.

Leaf 'n' Petal

Nadeau

Oak Street Garden Shop

Paper Source

Pottery Barn

Smith's Variety

Sur La Table

Table Matters

Target

Tricia's Treasures

West Elm

Williams-Sonoma

World Market

## *Thanks to the following homeowners*

Patsy & Matt Aiken

Crawford & Stephen Bumgarner

Katherine & John Cobbs

Elizabeth & James Outland

Ms. Ellen Stuart

# GENERAL INDEX

# METRIC EQUIVALENTS

*The recipes that appear in this cookbook use the standard United States method for measuring liquid and dry or solid ingredients (teaspoons, tablespoons, and cups). The information in the following charts is provided to help cooks outside the U.S. successfully use these recipes. All equivalents are approximate.*

### Metric Equivalents for Different Types of Ingredients

A standard cup measure of a dry or solid ingredient will vary in weight depending on the type of ingredient. A standard cup of liquid is the same volume for any type of liquid. Use the following chart when converting standard cup measures to grams (weight) or milliliters (volume).

| Standard Cup | Fine Powder (ex. flour) | Grain (ex. rice) | Granular (ex. sugar) | Liquid Solids (ex. butter) | Liquid (ex. milk) |
|---|---|---|---|---|---|
| 1 | 140 g | 150 g | 190 g | 200 g | 240 ml |
| 3/4 | 105 g | 113 g | 143 g | 150 g | 180 ml |
| 2/3 | 93 g | 100 g | 125 g | 133 g | 160 ml |
| 1/2 | 70 g | 75 g | 95 g | 100 g | 120 ml |
| 1/3 | 47 g | 50 g | 63 g | 67 g | 80 ml |
| 1/4 | 35 g | 38 g | 48 g | 50 g | 60 ml |
| 1/8 | 18 g | 19 g | 24 g | 25 g | 30 ml |

### Useful Equivalents for Liquid Ingredients by Volume

| | | | | | | | | | | | | |
|---|---|---|---|---|---|---|---|---|---|---|---|---|
| 1/4 tsp | | | | | | | | = | 1 ml | | |
| 1/2 tsp | | | | | | | | = | 2 ml | | |
| 1 tsp | | | | | | | | = | 5 ml | | |
| 3 tsp | = | 1 Tbsp | | | = | 1/2 fl oz | | = | 15 ml | | |
| | | 2 Tbsp | = | 1/8 cup | = | 1 fl oz | | = | 30 ml | | |
| | | 4 Tbsp | = | 1/4 cup | = | 2 fl oz | | = | 60 ml | | |
| | | 5 1/3 Tbsp | = | 1/3 cup | = | 3 fl oz | | = | 80 ml | | |
| | | 8 Tbsp | = | 1/2 cup | = | 4 fl oz | | = | 120 ml | | |
| | | 10 2/3 Tbsp | = | 2/3 cup | = | 5 fl oz | | = | 160 ml | | |
| | | 12 Tbsp | = | 3/4 cup | = | 6 fl oz | | = | 180 ml | | |
| | | 16 Tbsp | = | 1 cup | = | 8 fl oz | | = | 240 ml | | |
| | | 1 pt | = | 2 cups | = | 16 fl oz | | = | 480 ml | | |
| | | 1 qt | = | 4 cups | = | 32 fl oz | | = | 960 ml | | |
| | | | | | | 33 fl oz | | = | 1000 ml | = | 1 l |

### Useful Equivalents for Dry Ingredients by Weight

(To convert ounces to grams, multiply the number of ounces by 30.)

| | | | | |
|---|---|---|---|---|
| 1 oz | = | 1/16 lb | = | 30 g |
| 4 oz | = | 1/4 lb | = | 120 g |
| 8 oz | = | 1/2 lb | = | 240 g |
| 12 oz | = | 3/4 lb | = | 360 g |
| 16 oz | = | 1 lb | = | 480 g |

### Useful Equivalents for Length

(To convert inches to centimeters, multiply the number of inches by 2.5.)

| | | | | | | | | |
|---|---|---|---|---|---|---|---|---|
| 1 in | | | | | = | 2.5 cm | | |
| 6 in | = | 1/2 ft | | | = | 15 cm | | |
| 12 in | = | 1 ft | | | = | 30 cm | | |
| 36 in | = | 3 ft | = | 1 yd | = | 90 cm | | |
| 40 in | | | | | = | 100 cm | = | 1 m |

### Useful Equivalents for Cooking/Oven Temperatures

| | Fahrenheit | Celsius | Gas Mark |
|---|---|---|---|
| Freeze water | 32° F | 0° C | |
| Room temperature | 68° F | 20° C | |
| Boil water | 212° F | 100° C | |
| Bake | 325° F | 160° C | 3 |
| | 350° F | 180° C | 4 |
| | 375° F | 190° C | 5 |
| | 400° F | 200° C | 6 |
| | 425° F | 220° C | 7 |
| | 450° F | 230° C | 8 |
| Broil | | | Grill |

# RECIPE INDEX

135 West 50th Street, New York, NY 10020



ISBN-13: 978-0-8487-4335-2
ISBN-10: 0-8487-4335-0
ISSN: 0747-7791



Printed in the United States of America
First Printing 2014

**Oxmoor House**
Vice President, Brand Publishing: Laura Sappington
Editorial Director: Leah McLaughlin
Creative Director: Felicity Keane
Art Director: Christopher Rhoads
Senior Brand Manager: Daniel Fagan
Senior Editor: Rebecca Brennan
Managing Editor: Elizabeth Tyler Austin
Assistant Managing Editor: Jeanne de Lathouder

## *Christmas with Southern Living 2014*
Editor: Susan Hernandez Ray
Project Editors: Emily Chappell Connolly, Lacie Pinyan
Senior Designer: Melissa Clark
Executive Food Director: Grace Parisi
Assistant Test Kitchen Manager: Alyson Moreland Haynes
Recipe Developers and Testers: Wendy Ball, R.D.; Tamara Goldis, R.D.; Stefanie Maloney; Callie Nash; Karen Rankin; Leah Van Deren
Food Stylists: Victoria E. Cox, Margaret Monroe Dickey, Catherine Crowell Steele
Photography Director: Jim Bathie
Senior Photographer: Hélène Dujardin
Senior Photo Stylists: Kay E. Clarke, Mindi Shapiro Levine
Assistant Photo Stylist: Mary Louise Menendez
Senior Production Managers: Greg A. Amason, Sue Chodakiewicz

Cover: Red Velvet Marble Bundt Cake, page 82

Back Cover: Pork with Apples, Bacon, and Sauerkraut, page 126; Run for the Roses, page 21; Red Velvet-Raspberry Tiramisù Trifle, page 81

**Contributors**
Editor: Katherine Cobbs
Designer: Carol Damsky
Recipe Editor: Ashley Strickland Freeman
Recipe Developer and Tester: Jan Smith
Copy Editor: Donna Baldone
Proofreader: Adrienne Davis
Indexer: Mary Ann Laurens
Fellows: Ali Carruba, Frances Higginbotham, Elizabeth Laseter, Amy Pinney, Madison Taylor Pozzo, Deanna Sakal, April Smitherman, Megan Thompson, Tonya West
Food Stylist: Marian Cooper Cairns
Food Stylist Assistant: Angela Schmidt
Photographers: Iain Bagwell, Beau Gustafson, Becky Luigart-Stayner
Photo Stylists: Mary Clayton Carl, Susan Huff, Lydia DeGaris Pursell

## *Southern Living*®
Editor: M. Lindsay Bierman
Creative Director: Robert Perino
Managing Editor: Candace Higginbotham
Executive Editors: Hunter Lewis, Jessica S. Thuston
Deputy Food Director: Whitney Wright
Senior Food Editor: Julie Grimes
Test Kitchen Director: Robby Melvin
Test Kitchen Specialist/Food Styling: Vanessa McNeil Rocchio
Test Kitchen Professional: Pam Lolley
Recipe Editor: JoAnn Weatherly
Assistant Editor: Hannah Hayes
Style Director: Heather Chadduck Hillegas
Director of Photography: Jeanne Dozier Clayton
Photographers: Robbie Caponetto, Laurey W. Glenn, Hector Sanchez
Assistant Photo Editor: Kate Phillips Robertson
Photo Coordinator: Chris Ellenbogen
Senior Photo Stylist: Buffy Hargett Miller
Assistant Photo Stylist: Caroline M. Cunningham
Photo Administrative Assistant: Courtney Authement
Editorial Assistant: Pat York

**Time Home Entertainment Inc.**
President and Publisher: Jim Childs
Vice President, Brand & Digital Strategy: Steven Sandonato
Vice President, Finance: Vandana Patel
Executive Director, Marketing Services: Carol Pittard
Executive Director, Retail & Special Sales: Tom Mifsud
Executive Publishing Director: Joy Butts
Publishing Director: Megan Pearlman
Director, Bookazine Development & Marketing: Laura Adam
Associate General Counsel: Helen Wan

# Holiday Planner

*This handy planner will help you stay on track all season long. From decorating and table setting tips to gift and card lists, everything you need to plan the perfect holiday is at your fingertips.*

# NOVEMBER 2014

| Sunday | Monday | Tuesday | Wednesday |
| --- | --- | --- | --- |
| | | | |
| 2 | 3 | 4 | 5 |
| 9 | 10 | 11 | 12 |
| 16 | 17 | 18 | 19 |
| 23 / 30 | 24 | 25 | 26 |

| Thursday | Friday | Saturday |
|---|---|---|
| | | 1 |
| 6 | 7 | 8 |
| 13 | 14 | 15 |
| 20 | 21 | 22 |
| Thanksgiving 27 | 28 | 29 |

# A HEAD START ON THE HOLIDAYS

*Use this checklist for a smooth start to the season.*

## Deep-Clean your Home

- ☐ Make time to scrub every nook and cranny so you won't have to stress when guests pop in and out around Christmas.
- ☐ Go through old and current clothing, shoes, and other items. Make a pile for those you don't want and plan to donate them to Goodwill or another worthy cause in December.

## Plan your Gifts

- ☐ Make a list of gift recipients, plus everything you will need to buy.
- ☐ Many stores have post-Thanksgiving sales, making this the perfect time to start your Christmas shopping.
- ☐ Stock up on wrapping paper, bows, gift bags, boxes, and tags.

## Fill Up the Freezer

- ☐ Now is the perfect time to cook your family's favorite chili, pasta sauce, or stew recipes. You'll thank yourself later when you're busy with last-minute Christmas tasks.

## Make a Holiday Party Plan

- ☐ Decide what type of party you want to have, whether it's a holiday tea or cookie swap, then establish a budget and create a guest list.
- ☐ Start a shopping list, and include everything from food to decorations. Make arrangements if you will need to rent equipment or book a venue.

## Count Down with an Advent Calendar

- ☐ This is a great way to get everyone excited about Christmas. Plan to reveal each day's surprise in December as a family.
- ☐ Opt for a traditional chocolate-filled advent calendar, or try something more inventive—Lego makes a fun version. Or, browse Pinterest for inspiration and make your own!

# DECEMBER 2014

| Sunday | Monday | Tuesday | Wednesday |
|---|---|---|---|
| | 1 | 2 | 3 |
| 7 | 8 | 9 | 10 |
| 14 | 15 | 16 | 17 |
| 21 | 22 | 23 | Christmas Eve 24 |
| 28 | 29 | 30 | New Year's Eve 31 |

| Thursday | Friday | Saturday |
| --- | --- | --- |
| 4 | 5 | 6 |
| 11 | 12 | 13 |
| 18 | 19 | 20 |
| Christmas 25 | Boxing Day 26 | 27 |
| | | |

# SET THE PERFECT HOLIDAY TABLE

*Stay traditional or make a statement with your table setting—it's up to you! Here are some ideas to get you started:*

## Winter Wonderland

- ☐ Light white candles on a white tablecloth, and scatter glittery snowflakes around miniature artificial snow-dusted Christmas trees to create a whimsical setting.

## Red and Gold

- ☐ Break from the traditional reds and greens and adorn your table with bold shades of reds and golds. A deep red tablecloth paired with a gold runner creates a dramatic effect.

## Rustic

- ☐ A centerpiece of pinecones, holly branches, and other greenery over a burlap table runner creates a natural, wooded effect. Leave off the tablecloth on wooden tables to expose their beautiful finishes.

## DIY Christmas

- ☐ Put your imagination to work, and craft your own table setting. Create napkin holders by gluing red pom-poms onto green felt cut in the shape of a holly leaf. You can also garnish a silver ring with a piece of greenery. For kids, slip a napkin through a miniature slinky to make them smile.
- ☐ Make your own holiday poppers with toilet paper tubes, cracker snaps, wrapping paper, and ribbons. (Look online for detailed step-by-step guides.) Fill them with candy, novelty toys, silly riddles, or whatever you want—your guests will love them!

# DECORATING PLANNER

Here's a list of details and finishing touches you can use to tailor a picture-perfect house this holiday season.

## Decorative materials needed

from the yard ..............................................................................................................

..............................................................................................................................

from around the house...................................................................................................

..............................................................................................................................

from the store ..............................................................................................................

..............................................................................................................................

other.............................................................................................................................

## Holiday decorations

for the table ..................................................................................................................

..............................................................................................................................

for the door ...................................................................................................................

..............................................................................................................................

for the mantel ...............................................................................................................

..............................................................................................................................

for the staircase.............................................................................................................

..............................................................................................................................

other.............................................................................................................................

## DRESS UP YOUR POINSETTIAS

*The quintessential Christmas plant, the poinsettia's colorful leaves add a splash of color to any mantel or table setting.*

**Poinsettias for Decorating and Giving**

• Arrange cut poinsettias in tall, clear vases along your mantel or windowsill to create a focal point in your living room, dining room, or kitchen.

• For a vibrant centerpiece, place cut poinsettias in glass trifles or stands on your dining room table.

• Red is the most popular color, but poinsettias also come in ivory, shades of pink, orange, and in multicolored varieties. Try contrasting various colors next to each other in your home.

• Poinsettias also come in miniature varieties, which make great gifts for friends, neighbors, and teachers.

**Poinsettia Pointers**

• Poinsettias don't take well to cold weather, especially frost. Keep them inside at temperatures from 60° to 70°. Mist poinsettias daily if the air inside your home is dry.

• Poinsettias prefer indirect sunlight, so place them near a window or in a well-lit room of your home.

• If you plan to cut and arrange poinsettias, sear the stems to keep blossoms perky and fresh. Place the end of the stem over a candle flame immediately after cutting it from the plant. The sap from the stem should bubble as you hold it in the flame.
If done properly, you will have perky poinsettias!

# A CRAFTY CHRISTMAS

Read on for our favorite DIY projects that the entire family will love.

## MAKE A MASON JAR SNOW GLOBE

***Supplies you'll need:***

**Superglue**

**Plastic ornaments, figurines, or toys**

**Mason jars**

**Water**

**Liquid glycerin (available at craft stores)**

**Glitter**

**1.** Glue the ornament to the underside of the jar's lid. Let dry.

**2.** Fill the jar with water until the ornament is completely submerged. Add three to five drops of glycerin, then add desired amount of glitter to jar.

**3.** Glue the lid to the metal screw band. Let dry.

**4.** Apply glue to the inside band of the lid, then screw onto the jar. Let dry completely before shaking.

---

## MAKE A GINGERBREAD HOUSE

***Supplies you'll need:***

**Royal Icing**

**2 (16-oz.) packages powdered sugar**

**6 Tbsp. meringue powder (available at cake supply and craft stores)**

**6 to 8 Tbsp. warm water**

**1 (14.4-oz.) box graham crackers**

**Glitter, jimmies (assorted colors)**

**Gumdrops, candy canes, and your favorite candies**

**1.** Make Royal Icing: Beat powdered sugar, meringue powder, and 6 Tbsp. warm water at low speed with an electric mixer until blended. Beat at high speed 4 minutes or until stiff peaks form. Add up to 2 Tbsp. more warm water, ¼ tsp. at a time, until desired consistency is reached. Spoon into a plastic zip-top freezer bag, and snip off 1 corner to make a piping bag.

**2.** Hold 2 full graham cracker sheets vertically and carefully saw the sides of 2 more graham crackers to create downward slanting edges at the top. This will be the front and back of your house.

**3.** Hold 2 more full graham cracker sheets horizontally, and pipe Royal Icing along the short edges. These are the sides of your house.

**4.** On a work surface or plate, attach the first 2 graham crackers to the 2 shorter, and cut crackers to make a rectangle, sealing each end with piped Royal Icing. Now your house has a base.

**5.** To make the roof, pipe Royal Icing along slanted edges of the taller graham crackers, and attach 1 full sheet on each side to create the roof.

**6.** Attach desired decorations with Royal Icing.

# PARTY **PLANNER**

Stay on top of your party plans with our time-saving menu organizer.

| GUESTS | WHAT THEY'RE BRINGING | SERVING PIECES NEEDED |
| --- | --- | --- |
| | ☐ appetizer ☐ beverage ☐ bread ☐ main dish ☐ side dish ☐ dessert | |
| | ☐ appetizer ☐ beverage ☐ bread ☐ main dish ☐ side dish ☐ dessert | |
| | ☐ appetizer ☐ beverage ☐ bread ☐ main dish ☐ side dish ☐ dessert | |
| | ☐ appetizer ☐ beverage ☐ bread ☐ main dish ☐ side dish ☐ dessert | |
| | ☐ appetizer ☐ beverage ☐ bread ☐ main dish ☐ side dish ☐ dessert | |
| | ☐ appetizer ☐ beverage ☐ bread ☐ main dish ☐ side dish ☐ dessert | |
| | ☐ appetizer ☐ beverage ☐ bread ☐ main dish ☐ side dish ☐ dessert | |
| | ☐ appetizer ☐ beverage ☐ bread ☐ main dish ☐ side dish ☐ dessert | |
| | ☐ appetizer ☐ beverage ☐ bread ☐ main dish ☐ side dish ☐ dessert | |
| | ☐ appetizer ☐ beverage ☐ bread ☐ main dish ☐ side dish ☐ dessert | |
| | ☐ appetizer ☐ beverage ☐ bread ☐ main dish ☐ side dish ☐ dessert | |
| | ☐ appetizer ☐ beverage ☐ bread ☐ main dish ☐ side dish ☐ dessert | |
| | ☐ appetizer ☐ beverage ☐ bread ☐ main dish ☐ side dish ☐ dessert | |
| | ☐ appetizer ☐ beverage ☐ bread ☐ main dish ☐ side dish ☐ dessert | |
| | ☐ appetizer ☐ beverage ☐ bread ☐ main dish ☐ side dish ☐ dessert | |
| | ☐ appetizer ☐ beverage ☐ bread ☐ main dish ☐ side dish ☐ dessert | |

## Party Guest List

## Grocery List

## Party To-Do List

# CHRISTMAS DINNER PLANNER

Use this space to create a menu, to-do list, and guest list for your special holiday celebration.

## Menu Ideas

## Dinner To-Do List

## Christmas Dinner Guest List

# HOW TO STOCK A BAR

Bring back happy hour!

## PLAN AHEAD

Add cheer to any holiday gathering with a well-planned bar. Store spirits on a tray that slides easily in and out of your liquor cabinet for a grab-and-go setup. Make note of what needs replenishing after every party, and purchase it before you need it so that you are always prepared.

## THE BASICS

A great party doesn't require an extensive bar offering or even an exotic one. Simply put, you must make sure that you can supply all the basic ingredients required for your guests' drinks. Covering the basics just takes advanced planning and some simple math to determine the amounts needed.

## MAKE IT PRETTY

Instead of the standard white tablecloth-covered card table, go the extra mile. For pizzazz, drape the table with brightly colored fabric, or use a vintage bar cart for a more retro serving station. Dress up drinks with fruit-juice ice cubes or colored salt and sugar rims. Serve wine from pretty decanters rather than directly from the bottle.

Place a fresh flower arrangement on the bar. Offer wine glass charms or beer bands to help guests remember whose cocktail is whose, and set out napkins to prevent drink rings on furniture. Identify premixed or decanted drinks with decorative labels to let guests know what is what.

## GLASSES, CUPS, ETC.

Plastic cups, crystal stemware, and ruby-tinted martini glasses are all okay depending on the style, theme, and time of your party. If your party is formal, opt for crystal. If it's more casual, choose plastic. Traditionally, white and red wines are served in different types of glasses (narrower for whites, wider for reds so that they can breathe).

However, there is no actual rule requiring you to serve beverages in any certain type of glass, but offering a selection of glasses will add more sophistication to your bar. Stock up on inexpensive sets of a variety of wine glasses, martini glasses, pilsners, and Champagne flutes that you store for festive occasions, and consider sharing the cost and use with a friend.

## ICE ADVICE

A good rule of thumb for any party is to have anywhere between a half pound to one pound of ice per person. That may sound like a lot, but remember that you may need ice to fill an ice chest on the back porch, to blend with frozen mixes, and to serve cocktails on the rocks.

Buy bags of ice and store them in an ice chest on the deck, or, for smaller parties, empty the ice from your freezer's ice maker into an extra container in your freezer the night before to allow double ice storing and production capacity. Ice typically comes in five-pound bags; determine how many bags you will need before you head to the store. Don't forget to put a cooler in your car to keep your ice frozen solid.

## ESTIMATING POURS

Purchase at least half a bottle of wine per person for any gathering, but err on the generous side. Think about how your event is planned. Is it a sit-down dinner party or a reception? Adjust drink expectations accordingly.

A standard bottle has about five 5-ounce servings, so we suggest 4 glasses for brunch (1 for appetizers, 2 for entrée, 1 for dessert), 3 to 4 glasses for a cocktail party, 1 bottle per person for an evening buffet, and 6 glasses for a dinner party (2 glasses for appetizers, 3 for entrée, and 1 for dessert). Half a bottle per person may sound like a lot, but remember that you know your guests best. Buy more or less depending on your crowd.

## POPPING THE CORK

If you're serving only red and white wine, make sure there's enough of each and that they're at the right temperature. Chill white wines in the fridge or a wine chiller. Open red wines early to allow them to breathe. Two things to keep in mind about wine: Red keeps well, so don't worry about over-purchasing, and retailers may allow you to return unopened, unchilled white wines. When pouring, fill glasses just under the halfway mark.

# GIFTS AND GREETINGS

Keep up with family & friends' sizes, jot down gift ideas, and record purchases in this convenient chart. Also, use it to keep track of addresses for your Christmas card list.

## Gift List and Size Charts

**NAME/SIZES** **GIFT PURCHASED/MADE** **SENT**

name ..........

jeans_____ shirt_____ sweater_____ jacket_____ shoes_____ belt___
blouse_____ skirt_____ slacks_____ dress_____ suit_____ coat_____
pajamas_____ robe_____ hat_____ gloves_____ ring_____

name ..........

jeans_____ shirt_____ sweater_____ jacket_____ shoes_____ belt___
blouse_____ skirt_____ slacks_____ dress_____ suit_____ coat_____
pajamas_____ robe_____ hat_____ gloves_____ ring_____

name ..........

jeans_____ shirt_____ sweater_____ jacket_____ shoes_____ belt___
blouse_____ skirt_____ slacks_____ dress_____ suit_____ coat_____
pajamas_____ robe_____ hat_____ gloves_____ ring_____

name ..........

jeans_____ shirt_____ sweater_____ jacket_____ shoes_____ belt___
blouse_____ skirt_____ slacks_____ dress_____ suit_____ coat_____
pajamas_____ robe_____ hat_____ gloves_____ ring_____

name ..........

jeans_____ shirt_____ sweater_____ jacket_____ shoes_____ belt___
blouse_____ skirt_____ slacks_____ dress_____ suit_____ coat_____
pajamas_____ robe_____ hat_____ gloves_____ ring_____

name ..........

jeans_____ shirt_____ sweater_____ jacket_____ shoes_____ belt___
blouse_____ skirt_____ slacks_____ dress_____ suit_____ coat_____
pajamas_____ robe_____ hat_____ gloves_____ ring_____

name ..........

jeans_____ shirt_____ sweater_____ jacket_____ shoes_____ belt___
blouse_____ skirt_____ slacks_____ dress_____ suit_____ coat_____
pajamas_____ robe_____ hat_____ gloves_____ ring_____

# Christmas Card List

| NAME | ADDRESS | SENT |
| --- | --- | --- |

# HOLIDAY MEMORIES

Hold on to priceless Christmas memories forever with handwritten recollections of this season's magical moments.

## Treasured Traditions

**Keep track of your family's favorite holiday customs and pastimes on these lines.**

## Special Holiday Activities

**What holiday events do you look forward to year after year? Write them down here.**

## Holiday Visits and Visitors

**Keep a list of this year's holiday visitors. Jot down friend and family news as well.**

## This Year's Favorite Recipes

**Appetizers and Beverages**

**Entrées**

**Sides and Salads**

**Cookies and Candies**

**Desserts**

# LOOKING AHEAD

## Holiday Wrap-up

**Use this checklist to record thank-you notes sent for holiday gifts and hospitality.**

| NAME | GIFT AND/OR EVENT | NOTE SENT |
|---|---|---|
| | | ☐ |
| | | ☐ |
| | | ☐ |
| | | ☐ |
| | | ☐ |
| | | ☐ |
| | | ☐ |
| | | ☐ |
| | | ☐ |
| | | ☐ |
| | | ☐ |
| | | ☐ |
| | | ☐ |

## Notes for Next Year

**Write down your ideas for Christmas 2015 on the lines below.**

6-14